need to know?

Christianity

Peter Graystone

Collins

All Bible references are from the 2001 edition of the
New International Version, published by Hodder & Stoughton.

First published in 2008 by Collins
an imprint of
HarperCollins Publishers
77–85 Fulham Palace Road
London w6 8jb

www.collins.co.uk

A catalogue record for this book is available from
the British Library

Text: Peter Graystone
Editor: Grapevine Publishing Services
Designer: Bob Vickers
Series design: Mark Thomson
Front cover photograph: Corbis
Back cover photographs: Corbis

ISBN 978-0-00-7261161

Colour reproduction by Colourscan, Singapore
Printed and bound by Printing Express Ltd,
Hong Kong

Contents

To Nigel, with thanks

Introduction

No matter what they disagree about, all the Christians of the world agree about three straightforward things. Firstly, there is a God. Secondly, in a way so unique that it is beyond human understanding, God touched this planet 2000 years ago in the person of Jesus. And thirdly, that matters!

Christian faith is no longer central to the lives of men and women in the UK. Ninety-nine per cent of the population will see the outside of a church this week, but only 7 per cent will see the inside of one. For many, Christianity represents something irrelevant or just boring. For some it represents a threat. But whether we acknowledge it or not, the legacy of Jesus has fundamentally shaped the way we think, work and relate to one another.

Over the course of twenty centuries Christianity has moulded the culture, morality and way of life of a very large proportion of the world. This book tells the story of how the followers of Jesus came to shape the world in which we live. It explains the most important beliefs and practices of Christians the world over. And it analyses the state of Christianity around the globe today – not only in the UK, where worshippers are leaking away from the churches, but also in the developing world, where churches are growing at about ten times the rate at which they are declining in Europe.

For 2000 years Christianity has been responsible for some of the greatest movements to influence humankind for good. It has also been the cause of appalling bloodshed. World-changing triumph and neighbour-serving humility both feature in its story. But through it all, millions and millions of people have discovered that, because they have allowed the presence of Jesus to become a reality to them, they are glad to be alive.

This is a book about a God who offers to enrich and fulfil human lives. Enjoy it!

1 Jesus

Just over 2000 years ago a boy was born to a Jewish family in the part of the world that is now shared uneasily by Israel and the Palestinian Territories. Like many other would-be leaders of the time, he announced a vision for a world driven by love and justice, gathered a large following and suffered a humiliating and early death. Unlike others of the time, twenty centuries later he is worshipped by countless followers who believe him to be God. This chapter tells the remarkable story of Jesus and explains how he came to be known as Christ.

The life of Jesus

The faith that is practised by one third of the people on our planet began with a skirmish. In Nazareth, a town 65 miles north of Jerusalem, a Jewish travelling preacher who was making a name for himself in the vicinity gave his first sermon in the synagogue. His name was Jesus.

must know

Most of what is known about the life of Jesus comes from four biographies preserved in the Bible. Called gospels, they are named after four people associated with Jesus, although their actual authors are unknown. There are also brief references to Jesus in other writings of the time, and several accounts of Jesus' life that are so sensational that Christians a century later decided they were too far-fetched to include in the Bible.

Jesus' manifesto

Jesus spent his childhood years in Nazareth, where he was brought up in a craftsman's family, so there was local pride in the name he was making for himself as a rousing speaker.

Jesus' first recorded sermon was a manifesto for a kingdom in which poverty would be eradicated, oppression brought to an end, and the pleasure God takes in his people proclaimed. The Jewish people were ruled from afar by an emperor who used military might to suppress all opposition – Tiberius Caesar in Rome. So Jesus' vision was thoroughly welcome.

The beginning of the sermon was greeted with enthusiasm. However, Jesus went on to say something far more controversial. God's special relationship with men and women was no longer going to be exclusive to the Jewish people; other races were to be included in God's plan of love and healing for humankind. What's more, the Jews never had been the exclusive objects of God's love, and he could quote stories from Jewish history to prove it.

It was incendiary. The furious congregation rushed on the preacher with the intention of throwing him to his death over a precipice. But Jesus succeeded in fighting them off, fled through the middle of the mob and made off.

Jesus' ministry

This was the start of an extraordinary and traumatic ministry. Followers gathered eagerly around Jesus. At the height of his popularity they numbered thousands. Broken people found hope, suffering people experienced healing, brutalized people glimpsed the possibility of justice, and for three glorious years there was wonder in the air.

All too good to last! The popularity that was leading people to acclaim Jesus as a potential king was threatening to both political and religious leaders. It led to an end that seemed inevitable – arrest, trial and execution. It had happened to hundreds before him and it appeared that Jesus' death was one more tragedy in a savage generation.

However, something unprecedented happened. Within days, the followers of Jesus began to announce that, despite having witnessed his death, they had subsequently met with him. They believed that it was no vision or ghost that had transformed their demoralized group, but that their leader had been raised in a unique way from the dead.

The resurrection of Jesus inspired them to fulfil his manifesto – good news for the poor and spiritual renewal for the lost of every nation in the world. What is more, they began to proclaim that, in Jesus, God himself had been walking among them as a human. They did not just admire him as inspirational; they worshipped him as divine.

It was the beginning of Christianity.

> **must know**
>
> The four gospels are called Matthew, Mark, Luke and John. They were written between 30 and 70 years after Jesus' death. Gospel means 'good news'.

Early years

Mark, which was the first gospel to be written, makes no mention of Jesus' life before the age of 30. It may be that it was only as the eyewitnesses were dying out that it became important to investigate where and how Jesus was born. The research into Jesus' birth that went into Matthew's and Luke's accounts brought together study of the Jewish scriptures (the part of the Bible that Christians know as the Old Testament) and the recollections of those who knew Jesus.

The Jewish scriptures looked forward to a leader uniquely chosen by God (called the Christ or the Messiah – the words mean the same). They associated the birth of this Messiah with the ancestral line of David (the most respected king in the nation's history), with Bethlehem (David's birthplace) and with a virgin whose first child would be known as Emmanuel. The family of Jesus, however, was associated with Nazareth (some 70 miles away) and his parents were known to be Mary and Joseph.

All these facts came together to create an account that involved the young Mary (engaged but not yet married to Joseph) being visited in Nazareth by Gabriel, an angel. She was told that she had been chosen by the Lord to bear a son through whom God would be with his people in a unique way. She was to call him Jesus. Due to the godliness of Joseph, Mary was rescued from the disgrace associated with being pregnant and unmarried in that community. And because Joseph's forebears came from Bethlehem she gave birth in that town, because he was obliged to go there to register in a census.

must know

- Jesus means 'God saves'.
- Messiah and Christ both mean 'the Anointed One' (the first is a Hebrew word and the second is Greek).
- Emmanuel means 'God is with us'.
- 'Gentiles' was how the Jews, believing themselves to be God's chosen people, described all races and nationalities except their own.

Luke's gospel, which repeatedly stresses Jesus' compassion for marginalized people, records him being visited as a baby by local riff-raff (shepherds, drawn to Jesus by a vision of angels). Matthew's different account, by a Jew who stressed that Jesus' mission had no national boundaries, records him being visited as a toddler by foreign intellectuals (drawn to Jesus by astrological studies). It is the events of Jesus' birth that Christians rejoice in at Christmas, exchanging presents to recall gifts presented by those wise men.

According to Matthew, these events were overshadowed by tragedy. In Jerusalem, Herod the Great, whom the occupying Roman powers acknowledged as a politically convenient 'King of the Jews', felt threatened by rumours of the birth of a rival. He had male infants in Bethlehem murdered in order to eliminate the threat, but his troops arrived too late to kill Jesus, whose family had sought refuge in Egypt.

Preparing the way

The ground in which Jesus' teaching flourished was prepared by a firebrand named John. He was Jesus' cousin, and he led a sensational religious revival in the bleak country by the River Jordan. Jewish writings of five centuries previously had anticipated that the revered, ancient prophet Elijah would reappear to herald the Christ who would then overthrow the enemies of the Jews. John dressed like Elijah, lived in the same primitive fashion, and roared his message with the same power.

John's teaching was that judgement was about to fall on the Jews unless they turned from sinful ways, asked for God's forgiveness, and pledged themselves to justice. Crowds flocked to see him, and in the river he baptized people who committed themselves to this way of life. Among them was the 30-year-old Jesus. This encounter with John the Baptist had a profound impact on Jesus. His baptism was a moment at which he became aware of God's immeasurable love for him – like a father and son. He proceeded to spend 40 days in the desert region – a time of isolation, fasting and spiritual wrestling. It was this period that shaped the ministry to which God was calling him.

John recognized something exceptional in Jesus. He had consistently denied that he himself was the Messiah, but told his inner circle that Jesus far surpassed him and was unique in God's plans. These men became Jesus' first followers.

When John fell foul of the authorities and was imprisoned, Jesus moved north and lived in Capernaum, closer to the region where he had grown up. This was the time of his sermon at Nazareth. As he preached in the towns around Lake Galilee, he gathered a reputation for being able to heal sick people. His followers began to make decisive moves to accompany him on his travelling mission. He chose twelve of them who became his closest confidants. These 'disciples' were a diverse group, including Peter (a fisherman who went on to lead the first church), James and John (for whom he developed a particular affection) and Judas (who played a key role in the events that finally led to Jesus' death). At certain points, Jesus' disciples were sent ahead of him to villages he intended to visit in order to publicize his arrival.

must know

Baptism was practised by the Jews and adopted by the Christians. It marked a complete change of life or religion. It originally involved being immersed completely in the water of a river. This was and is a symbol of death (the old life drowning as a new and better one begins) and of cleansing (sin washed away through God's mercy).

Power and controversy

All four gospels focus in most detail on the life of Jesus from the age of 30 to 33. During those years he travelled mainly through the countryside around Lake Galilee and his reputation as someone who could work miracles rose dramatically. These are described in three different ways, revealing them to have a meaning beyond just spectacular events:

- **Miraculous powers** emphasizes the control that Jesus had over disease, mental illness and nature – a man with leprosy was healed; a screaming and disturbed man was calmed; 5000 hungry people were fed with only a few fish and loaves of bread.
- **Wonders** describes the impact that Jesus' actions had on those who saw what he did – when a life-threatening storm was stilled his disciples were frightened and awed: 'Who is this? Even the wind and the waves obey him!'
- **Signs** is the word that John's gospel uses to stress that Jesus' miracles were intended to draw attention to something unique about him – when a blind man's sight was restored it was a sign that Jesus, 'The light of the world', had come to heal the spiritual blindness of those who did not recognize what God was doing.

In keeping with the medical understanding of the day, Jesus saw many of his healing miracles as casting evil spirits out of a person. Alongside the soaring popularity that this brought came controversy over the source of the power. Jesus' abilities were undeniable, but those who opposed him claimed that he done a deal with the devil (Satan, the source of all evil) to give him magic powers. But Jesus said that absolutely the reverse

must know

Over 30 miracles of Jesus are retold in detail, and more alluded to. Among them are:
- a boy being cured of epilepsy
- the healing of the paralysed servant of a Roman centurion
- water being turned into wine during a wedding banquet
- walking on the water of Lake Galilee to reach a boat in which Jesus' frightened disciples were fighting the waves.

was true. Miracles were happening because evil was in retreat and God was taking control of his world. In him, God had begun the all-out attack on evil that would eventually bring sickness, grief, poverty and hunger to a categorical end.

The compassion that drove Jesus' ministry was also shown in the company he kept. Having been brought up in the artisan classes, educated and intelligent, he turned his back on that and made his home among the poor. He befriended society's outsiders, such as tax collectors (despised as traitors by their fellow Jews because they had taken lucrative jobs from the occupying Roman regime). Jesus stayed single, kept on the move, defied convention, relied on others for food and shelter, trod a delicate line between friends in the brothel and friends in the synagogue, and inspired in people the belief that a world of justice was not only desirable but possible.

In the context of the time it is particularly unusual that he treated women with absolute respect. A small group of women followed him as closely as his twelve disciples, and were responsible for funding his ministry. Among them were Mary Magdalene, to whom he gave a new purpose after calming her from a mental illness, and Joanna, the wife of the manager of Herod's household. (Ironically the money that her husband earned by maintaining the ruler's centre of oppression was being redirected into good news for the lost.) All this activity was exhausting, and it was punctuated by times when Jesus would retreat alone to isolated places and pray.

want to know more?
You can read the accounts of Jesus' miracles described in this section by referring to these parts of the Bible:
• Mark 1:40-42.
• Mark 1:23-27.
• Luke 9:12-17.
• Mark 4:35-41.
• John 9:1-41.
• Luke 8:1-3.

Jesus' teaching

In one sense, Jesus was a typical Jewish teacher of the first century. Everything he taught was drenched in the laws and prophecies of Jewish scripture. His two key declarations – that his followers' love for God should be absolute and that they should regard every other human life as equally deserving of love as their own – both came directly from the Old Testament (as Christians today would call it).

Jesus the Jew

'I have not come to abolish the Law or the Prophets,' said Jesus, 'but to fulfil them.' His genius was to scrape away the grime that had accumulated around Jewish writings that were ancient even then, to reveal the love and justice of God dazzling beneath them. He did this by storytelling, by giving old ideas new substance and by exposing the way in which religious conventions can sometimes lose the godliness of their original purpose.

In his Gospel, Mark attempted to summarize the whole of Jesus' teaching in three sentences: 'The time has come. The Kingdom of God is near. Repent and believe the good news!' Those sound bites sum up all the main themes of Jesus' message, but need more explanation for readers twenty centuries later.

'The time has come'

Jesus announced that the moment when God would save his people, long awaited by the Jews, was imminent. For centuries the Jews had expected God to intervene decisively in human affairs, bringing to pass all that their prophets had anticipated. Such

must know

In the first ever sermon, Jesus' close friend Peter described him like this to an audience of Jews:
• Listen to this! Jesus of Nazareth was a man accredited by God to you by miracles, wonders and signs, which God did among you through him ... With the help of wicked people you put him to death by nailing him to the cross. But God raised him from the dead, freeing him from the agony of death, because it was impossible for death to keep its hold on him.

was their longing that it is easy to understand why they were captivated by a man who not only announced that the crux had come, but had the charisma to make it believable.

The moment when God would bring the destiny of the Jews to a climax was known as the Day of the Lord, and it was associated in Jewish literature with several figures – a humble shepherd, a despised servant, a triumphant warrior. By the time of Jesus the name Messiah or Christ was being used to bring all these ideas together. Most Jews presumed that the emergence of God's Messiah would involve the overthrow of Roman rule and the restoration of Israel's independence. It would usher in another age like the glory days when David was king.

Jesus rarely spoke of himself as the Messiah. When he was asked directly whether he was the one, he told people to look at what he did and make up their own minds. By doing this he distanced himself from those who conspired toward an armed rebellion against Caesar's occupation. Instead he identified himself most strongly with the Servant figure, who sacrificially gave all he had in order to improve the lives of the poor, to the point of suffering and death.

Jesus additionally referred to himself by the strange name Son of Man. This figure, also from the Old Testament, was a complete contrast to the Suffering Servant. Although by itself the phrase just meant 'ordinary bloke', in a dazzling Old Testament vision the Son of Man was raised, glorious and triumphant, to stand in front of the throne of God. Holding those two images of sacrifice and victory together was central to Jesus' explanation of how

must know

Jesus explained his ministry by reminding people of words that had been written by the prophet Isaiah five or more centuries earlier, including:
• 'Here is my Servant, whom I uphold,
my chosen one in whom I delight;
I will put my Spirit on him and he will bring justice to the nations.' (Isaiah 42:1)
• 'He was despised and rejected by others,
a man of sorrows and familiar with suffering.' (Isaiah 53:3)
• 'The Spirit of the Sovereign Lord is on me, because the Lord has anointed me
to preach good news to the poor.' (Isaiah 61:1)

the Day of the Lord had arrived. Jesus' followers ever since have seen themselves as successors to both – servants of a needy world in which they announce salvation in the name of Jesus; looking forward to the future time when God will bring human affairs to an end, with irreversible healing, as Jesus is universally recognized as Lord.

'The Kingdom of God is near'

The Kingdom of God is another concept that was present in Jewish tradition, but Jesus made it central to his teaching. He made the idea more radical and more immediate than anyone who had gone before. It was not a physical place (so it was not going to be achieved by driving out the Romans), nor was it a particular group of people (so no religious group could claim it for themselves). Rather it was the place where the rule of God the King is accepted, and his will for the world is obeyed.

Instead of defining the Kingdom, Jesus told stories (parables) that required his listeners to work out what it is like to have God as king:

• **It is like a treasure** that a man stumbles upon unexpectedly, so valuable that it is worth giving up everything else in order to obtain it.

• **It is like a vulnerable woman getting the justice she deserves** by sheer perseverance against the odds.

• **It is like a small seed** within which is the potential life of a huge tree in which birds find nourishment and shelter.

• **It is like a party invitation** that the celebrities have snubbed, so those who are poor or despised, in fact anyone at all, can feast instead.

must know

Jesus also described himself by alluding to words of the prophet Daniel that were equally ancient:
• 'In my vision at night I looked, and there before me was one like a Son of Man, coming with the clouds of heaven. He approached the Ancient of Days and was led into his presence. He was given authority, glory and sovereign power; all peoples, nations and peoples of every language worshipped him.' (Daniel 7:13,14)

Two of Jesus' parables have had an ongoing resonance with Christians through the centuries. In one, which is clearly meant to point to the love and forgiveness of God, a father watches his son leave home and squander his money. With money and friends gone, the boy sinks fast and ends up in a job so repellent that he is forced to take stock. He realizes that his only option is to return to his father, acknowledge that he has done wrong and ask for menial employment. The father, however, has been yearning to see his son again and, glimpsing him in the distance, is overwhelmed with love. He runs to meet him and after an emotional reunion the son gets not a job, but a party. This is sometimes known as the parable of the prodigal son.

In the other, Jesus attacks racism and makes it clear that God the king expects his subjects to have compassion with no limits. A man is robbed, beaten and left for dead. Neither of the two religious people who might be expected to help him are willing to get involved. Instead the person least likely to assist a first-century Jew – a man from loathed, neighbouring Samaria – is the one who rescues him. This story is known as the parable of the good Samaritan and the uncomfortable inference is that someone from another religion is just as capable of displaying God's love as those who feel that their relationship with him is exclusive.

Provocative teaching

It is no wonder that such teaching antagonized Jewish intellectuals. It was one of them who prompted the parable of the good Samaritan by asking who was the neighbour referred to in God's command to 'love your neighbour as yourself'. He was probably a Pharisee – a group united by a commitment to God through a scrupulous adherence to Judaism. Pharisees believed that the terrible things that had befallen the Jews were a result of people's failure to keep God's laws. Because several hundred years had passed since the laws were written down, they didn't cover every aspect of day-to-day life. So the Pharisees gave themselves the task of clarifying the laws to give regulations for every single area of someone's existence.

For example, all Jews knew that on the Sabbath, their weekly day of rest and worship, no work should be done. The Pharisees sought to improve the law by laying down precisely how far Jews were allowed to walk on a Sabbath before it ceased to be a necessity to get to the synagogue and started to be a labour from which one might profit. So when a Pharisee asked Jesus, 'Who is my neighbour?' the implication was, 'I want to love the right people, as duty demands.' Jesus found this attitude intolerable, provoking the Pharisees by doing things on the Sabbath that were clearly good and life-enhancing, even though they broke the prohibitions. And he exploded the theory that loving your neighbour involved opposing all non-Jews: 'Love your enemies and do good to those who hate you.'

In the Kingdom of God, people would do what is good not because they feared the consequences of doing wrong, but because they appreciated the beauty of doing what is right. 'A new command I give you,' said Jesus: 'Love one another. As I have loved you, so you must love one another.'

Jesus' insistence that God required not a change of behaviour, but a change of heart, is best seen in his teaching about money. Wealth is dangerous not because it is evil in itself, but because there is only room for one king in the Kingdom, and wealthy people are more inclined to enthrone visible money than invisible God. 'You cannot serve both God and Money,' he demanded. The most life-enhancing thing the wealthy could do was to give away their possessions to the poor and follow the way of Jesus, serving the true God. And as for the poor (both the financially poor and the spiritually poor), they are the ones who have real blessings, because the Kingdom of God is theirs – God is in unrivalled control of their lives.

'Repent and believe the good news!'

'Repent and believe' was the response that Jesus demanded to the fact that the Kingdom had been inaugurated. There was an irony at the heart of this appeal. In one sense it was the most challenging call to a change of life because it involved uncompromised sacrifice; in another sense it was effortless because God himself would do everything that was needed on behalf of those who asked for his mercy.

The challenge was a serious commitment to a selfless lifestyle. Being a disciple involved joining Jesus in his mission – an allegiance that took precedence even over family loyalties. It involved being noticeably different from others. Disciples were to be 'salt of the earth' – acting as a preservative to prevent corruption. They were to be 'the light of the world' – giving direction to a society in moral darkness. Seeping like salt or blazing like light, the very distinctiveness of their characters would change the culture for good.

As 'children of God' his disciples were to reflect their Father's characteristics – making peace, seeking justice ('righteousness'), displaying both mercy and purity. They were to be generous, loving others without making distinctions, and they were to obey God without question. Jesus anticipated that most of the world would find these ethical standards to be unnatural and unwelcome. In fact, he told his followers to expect to be persecuted because of them. They might even die as a result.

So why was it worthwhile to be a follower of Jesus? He presented himself as a leader of a completely different kind from any who had gone before. His commitment and his integrity were total. Picturing himself as 'the good shepherd' he pledged to know and care for his followers (his 'flock') with such devotion that other leaders would seem fraudulent by comparison. Previous leaders had self-serving objectives; Jesus had come so that his followers 'may have life, and have it to the full'.

Jesus assured his followers that they were going to be part of a new community, one so loving and supportive that it would more than compensate for any loss they suffered by turning their back on possessions or people that were inhibiting their progress toward the Kingdom of God. What is more, the outcome would be far more than an improvement to earthly life. The ultimate gain was 'eternal life', a relationship with the timeless God that would not end even at the point of death. The new life that the disciples of Jesus had embarked on was for ever.

Yet paradoxically, this eternal life that Jesus' followers could expect was not something that they would need to strive for arduously. It would not be earned by adherence to the rules involved in going the way of Jesus. Eternal life was God's gift to humanity. A painstaking effort to keep the letter of the law might even become an obstacle, as it had become for the Pharisees.

Such was the unconditional love (or 'grace') of God that he would accept anyone who came to him humble and helpless. The best model for a life of real value was a lowly child, unable to do anything for herself, but relying totally on someone else. 'I tell you the truth,' said Jesus, 'anyone who will not receive the kingdom of God like a little child will never enter it.' The younger and more helpless the child, the better for allowing God to create in her something new and good! God desired, in fact, to give humans a rebirth: 'I tell you the truth, no one can see the Kingdom of God without being born again.'

want to know more?
To read the sayings and parables of Jesus described in this section, refer to:
- Matthew 5:17.
- Mark 1:15.
- Matthew 13:44.
- Luke 18:1-8.
- Matthew 13:31,32.
- Luke 16:16-24.
- Luke 15:11-24.
- Luke 10:30-37.
- Luke 6:27.
- John 13:34.
- Matthew 6:24.
- Matthew 5:13-16.
- John 10:7-21.
- Luke 18:17.
- John 3:3.

The death of Jesus

During the third year of his mission, Jesus made a crucial decision. He could go to Galilee, where his popularity was greatest, or to Jerusalem, where the controversy would be fiercest. Jesus chose to go to the city, and set out resolutely, knowing that this would lead to conflict and death.

must know

The major events of Jesus' final week are marked by Christians every year – some with special church services, and some with national holidays. They are given particular names:

• Palm Sunday recalls Jesus' triumphant ride into Jerusalem.

• Maundy Thursday marks the meal at which Jesus asked his followers to remember him by eating bread and drinking wine together (the 'Last Supper').

• Good Friday is the day on which Christians remember Jesus' execution.

• Easter is celebrated with great joy to recall the Sunday when Jesus' tomb was found to be empty because he had risen from the dead.

Jesus' final week

Repeatedly, Jesus told his disciples that he anticipated being put to death. It would not be an accident, nor a tragedy – it was God's scheme. 'The Son of Man did not come to be served, but to serve', he said, 'and to give his life as a ransom for many.' It was as if Jesus' imminent death was the most important part of his life. He compared himself to a seed that has to be buried in order for a harvest to multiply. He saw himself as the central figure in a plan of God through which all the world would reap an incalculable benefit. Claiming for himself a uniquely close relationship with God as his Father, Jesus explained, 'God did not send his Son into the world to condemn the world, but to save the world through him.'

The governor whom the Roman authorities had placed in Jerusalem was named Pontius Pilate. He had a sadistic and confrontational approach to ruling the Jews. He had infuriated them by bringing military standards into Jerusalem (they bore the image of the Caesar, a man who claimed to be a god, which the Jews found utterly offensive to have near their holiest places). And he had terrorized them by having Jewish pilgrims, who had come to Jerusalem to celebrate their most important religious festival, Passover, butchered in their own temple.

It was Passover time again, so the city was packed with Jews. Pilate knew that tensions would be running high at the anniversary of this event. The Jews anticipated that when their Messiah made his move to overthrow the Romans and re-establish Jewish government, it would be during Passover. It is almost certain that Jesus' disciples, nervous and questioning as they followed him to Jerusalem, wondered whether this was the moment at which he would establish God's Kingdom by driving the Gentiles out of Jerusalem. But Jesus had other ideas.

For Pilate to ride into Jerusalem from his summer residence on the west coast, resplendent on a horse and surrounded by Roman soldiers, was a familiar sight. When Jesus entered Jerusalem it was from the east, he was surrounded by revelling Jewish pilgrims, and he was riding a donkey.

There is no doubt that Jesus arranged this in order to proclaim that he was the promised Messiah. Jewish writings that were six centuries old had pictured God's king arriving in his city on a donkey. But in parodying Pilate, Jesus was forcing the crowd, many of whom were already agog at Jesus' reputation, to a point of decision. Would they support the Kingdom that God had inaugurated, in which the suffering were healed, the poor heard good news and the oppressed went free? Or would they tolerate an empire where the vulnerable were oppressed by a distant emperor? Jesus was doing what the Messiah might have been predicted to do, but in an entirely unexpected way – unarmed and with a festival atmosphere.

must know

Passover was (and still is) a festival in which the Jews commemorated events some thirteen centuries before Jesus. At a time when they were enslaved to Egyptian oppressors, a miraculous intervention by God enabled them to escape. It was this 'ransom' that established them as a free nation. The religious ritual involved the sacrifice of a lamb. The timing of Jesus' death, during the Passover festival, appears to have been chosen by him to resonate with the death of an innocent creature that meant freedom for God's people.

In response, the crowd used words and actions that unmistakeably implied recognition of Jesus as their Messiah. They yelled, 'Hosanna!' which means, 'Now is the time for God to save us!' They ripped down the branches of olive trees and grabbed palm leaves from the marketplace, waving them as was traditional to accompany some of the ancient Jewish hymns (psalms) written for times of military triumph. And significantly, they used a symbol of submission that had historically been used to acclaim a man as their king – throwing their cloaks under his feet. Jesus reacted to all this not with bravado, but with tears. Entering Jerusalem (whose name means 'the city of peace') he foresaw that it would become a city not of peace, but of carnage.

Having issued a direct challenge to the Roman political leaders in the manner in which he entered the city, Jesus immediately proceeded to challenge the Jewish religious leaders. He went into the temple courtyard and began proclaiming his message to the worshippers. He taught that prayer to God was the free right of people of every nation, and illustrated it in the most provocative way by overturning the stalls of the traders. It has been suggested that the traders were making substantial profits by insisting that only approved goods, purchased within the walls of the temple, could be used in worship, and that they could only be bought with the temple's own coinage, exchanged with a steep commission. This exploitation could all be justified by the priests as guarding scriptural standards, but it outraged Jesus, who threw furniture and merchandise around furiously.

Jesus' following, already huge, was growing daily – a fact which deeply unsettled the Jewish leaders, but made it difficult for them to know how to intervene to stop it.

want to know more?

The accounts of Jesus' approach to his own death can be found at:
- Mark 10:45.
- John 12:22-27.
- John 3:17.
- Luke 19:28-44.

Thursday

Jesus spent his last days in the temple courtyard, where there was a mixed reaction to his prediction of a coming crisis in which the temple would be destroyed. Repeatedly critical of the religious authorities, he urged people to make a decisive choice for the Kingdom of God.

Like all Jewish people, Jesus marked the Passover festival with a meal. He gathered his disciples in the upstairs guest room of a sympathizer's house in the city. Two things happened during this meal that made it unlike any other Passover.

Firstly Jesus, who might have been expected to spend his last night on earth reiterating his leadership, instead shocked his friends by performing tasks that would usually be undertaken by a servant. He made them comfortable in preparation for the meal by washing their feet, muddy from walking through the unpaved streets. When they expressed surprise, Jesus told them that this was an example of how his followers were to live – taking a humble role in serving others.

Secondly, as the traditional Passover foods (lamb, herbs, unleavened bread, wine and so on) were being eaten with ritual prayers and a retelling of ancient Jewish stories, Jesus drew particular attention to two of the foods. He took the bread, thanked God for it, broke and shared it (which was not unusual). He then added, 'Take and eat; this is my body' (which was extraordinary). As they shared the Passover wine, he made the equally startling declaration that they were drinking his blood, which was being poured out so that sins could be forgiven. He told the group to repeat this whenever they met together in order to remember him (a command that Christians have obeyed ever since).

It was during this meal that Judas, who had been with Jesus throughout the three years of his ministry, made up his mind to hand Jesus over to the authorities. For reasons that have never satisfactorily been explained, he went to the Jewish leaders, advised them of the best moment to seize Jesus without the protection of the crowds, and accepted thirty silver coins as a reward.

Jesus left the Passover celebration and headed back toward the house where he was staying. His disciples followed and, with tension rising, some of them armed themselves. They went to a favourite garden called Gethsemane, to the east of the city walls. Jesus, knowing what was coming, prayed in torment to God that he would not have to suffer. His disciples had fallen asleep, so were not aware of the distress that ended with Jesus submitting to God's plan: 'Not my will, but yours be done.'

Judas arrived and greeted Jesus with what appeared to be affection, but was actually an indication to the soldiers who to arrest. When they seized him, Jesus did not resist and his terrified friends scattered.

Friday

After a night of aggression and mockery, Jesus was brought to the first of two trials in the early hours of Friday morning. The supreme court of the Jews (the Sanhedrin council) called witnesses in order to secure a conviction for blasphemy. Jesus, who was silent, evasive and

want to know more?

Read about:
• Jesus washing his friends' feet, in John 13:1-17
• Jesus' last supper, in Matthew 26:14-30
• the arrest of Jesus, in Mark 14:32-50
• the trials of Jesus, in Matthew 26:57-68 and 27:11-31
• Jesus' death, in Luke 23:26-46.

forthright in succession, appears to have been more in control of the questioning than the priests. The council pronounced a death sentence in response to Jesus' claims to be the Messiah and to be divine.

The Jewish court, however, did not have the legal authority to carry out the sentence and sent Jesus to the Roman governor to have it confirmed. That is how Jesus came face to face with Pilate, accused now not of blasphemy but of incitement to treason. Pilate, fascinated by Jesus and disdaining the Jewish leaders, made several attempts to save him. Thinking that it would satisfy the Jewish festival pilgrims, he offered to set Jesus free. However, rabble-rousers sympathetic to the Jewish elite had turned the crowds against Jesus, and they bayed for his blood. Washing his hands to distance himself from their decision, Pilate signed Jesus' death warrant.

In a repulsive parody of a coronation ceremony, soldiers made a crown out of a thorn bush and pretended to worship Jesus. Then they beat him, took him to a hill called Calvary, which was an execution site and crucified him. His recorded words during the six hours he hung on the cross display an astonishing restraint. He cried in despair, quoting from the psalms of the Old Testament. He called out to God, committing his spirit to his care. And remarkably, he spoke words of forgiveness to those who were murdering him: 'Father, forgive them, for they do not know what they are doing.'

must know

Jesus was in the hands of the Roman political leaders when he was executed. If he had been under the jurisdiction of the Jewish leaders he would have been stoned to death, but the Roman form of execution for treason, murder or escaping slavery was crucifixion.

In this most barbaric means of killing someone, a man (or woman) was first stripped, then subjected to degrading humiliation and flogged with whips. His outstretched arms were tied or nailed to a wooden beam, which he was forced to carry through the streets to the execution site. The beam carrying his body was hoisted and secured to a vertical stake or tree trunk, creating the cross shape that has become Christianity's most familiar symbol. The victim's feet were nailed to the post, and he was left to die amid the taunts of onlookers.

A crucified person could breathe only by heaving his body to an upright position. Death came when he no longer had the strength to lift himself, and so asphyxiated. Many thousands were put to death in this way. The process sometimes took several days, although Jesus' suffering seems mercifully to have lasted only six hours.

Jesus – risen from the dead

On the Sunday, 40 hours after they had seen Jesus die, his remaining eleven disciples were together, scared and distraught. Into their miserable morning burst a group of women. They had seen Jesus, but not dead in his tomb. He was alive!

Sunday

One of the Jewish leaders had dissented from the Sanhedrin council's decision to have Jesus killed. Appalled at what had happened, Joseph went to Pilate for permission to have Jesus buried with dignity. Unexpectedly, this was granted and Jesus was placed in a cave-like tomb, with a boulder rolled across the entrance. This was done in some haste on the Friday evening because Jews observed their holy day (the Sabbath) from sunset on that day. Knowing they could not perform the burial rites until the Sabbath was over, the friends of Jesus must have passed Saturday in numbed grief waiting for Sunday morning. However, at some point, in the dark and quiet behind the sealed tombstone, God raised Jesus from the dead.

None of the four gospels describe Jesus' resurrection, but they all recount its aftermath. Their accounts differ markedly, but they all begin with women from Jesus' inner circle approaching the tomb very early on the Sunday morning in order to embalm the body. Between them, the narratives describe an earthquake, the women's shock at finding the stone rolled away from the tomb, the shroud that had wrapped Jesus' corpse abandoned inside it and the appearance of an angel announcing that Jesus had risen from the dead.

must know

Up to 600 people, singly, in pairs or groups, are recorded as having encountered Jesus after his resurrection. The accounts can be read in Matthew 28:1-20; Mark 16:1-20; Luke 24:1-53; John 20:1-21:25 and 1 Corinthians 15:1-8. Witnesses of the appearances include:
• two followers of Jesus who were walking the road from Jerusalem to Emmaus
• a group of the remaining disciples in a locked room
• Thomas, one of the original twelve, who needed to touch Jesus' scars in order to be persuaded
• the disciples who had initially been fishermen, on a beach beside Lake Galilee.

In one account it is Mary Magdalene and a companion who first find the tomb empty. Mary is approached by a man whom she assumes to be a gardener. When he addresses her by name she realizes that it is Jesus and that he has risen.

Jesus' appearances to his followers lasted for nearly six weeks. Descriptions of Jesus at this time portray something unique. His was not simply a body that had returned to life, because he was able to come and go at will even in locked rooms. However, it was also more than a vision – Jesus was able to eat meals with them. He transcended all that his friends had known for the previous three years, and yet the scars of his suffering were still evident on his body. Even the witnesses of these events were confused by them, so worship and doubt went side by side.

At first the appearances were frightening, but believers increasingly found them reassuring. Jesus explained the true significance of his life, planned by God to bring forgiveness and change to humankind. In a final appearance on a hill outside Jerusalem, he challenged his followers to take his message worldwide, creating new disciples. This became known as Jesus' ascension, culminating in a promise that his presence would henceforth be equally real, but not visible. United with God, he would no longer merely accompany a few eyewitnesses: 'Surely I am with you always, to the very end of the age.' Jesus' followers anticipated that the end to which he referred was imminent. They expected it to be marked by Jesus' triumphant return, in the glorious style that befits the Christ establishing the Kingdom of God on earth as it is in heaven.

must know

Over the centuries, sceptics have offered different explanations for the phenomenon of Jesus' resurrection:
- Perhaps he survived his crucifixion.
- Perhaps the disciples stole the body from the tomb and subsequent appearances were just visions.
- Perhaps the contradictory nature of the accounts is typical of the way the truth is embellished as years go by.

In contrast, believers point to evidence that the events of the first Easter were unique and miraculous:
- Eyewitnesses were persuaded that a resurrection – not a resuscitation, apparition or cover-up – had taken place.
- A group of disciples, demoralized by the death of their hero, were transformed with astonishing speed.
- The day of the week that Jesus' followers regarded as holy changed at once from Saturday (which had been the Jewish Sabbath for two millennia) to Sunday, a change so profound that only an unprecedented event can account for it.

Who was Jesus?

The fishermen who became Jesus' closest friends began to follow him because he seemed an outstanding man. As inexplicable events took place, they asked, 'What kind of man is this?' Seven days after his resurrection, one of the twelve described Jesus as 'My Lord and my God'. So who was Jesus Christ?

Father and Son

Had Jesus announced, 'I am God,' he would have been chained up as a madman or murdered in an obscure village. Instead he tantalized people by leading them to the point at which they were forced to consider the possibility that he might be divine. For Jews, the idea of a man claiming to be God (as the Roman emperor did) was abhorrent.

Jesus referred to God as Father – not in itself controversial, as Jews saw their nation as much-loved children of God. But he implied an exclusive relationship. 'I and the Father are one,' he ventured on one occasion in Jerusalem, outraging the listening Jews who would have stoned him there and then had he not been both a quick thinker and a quick runner. In private with his disciples, Jesus was even more explicit: 'I am in the Father and the Father is in me ... believe it on the evidence of the miracles.'

want to know more?

Some of the statements of Jesus in which a claim to be God are implicit can be examined at:
- John 10:30-39.
- John 14:5-14.
- John 17:1-5.
- Luke 5:17-26.
- John 11:25-27.
- Matthew 11:25-30.
- Matthew 25:31-46.

Jesus and God

When Jesus' first followers – almost all Jewish – came to believe that Jesus was God, they were thinking the unthinkable. It was the only conclusion they could draw.

On one occasion a paralysed man was brought to Jesus by friends who were convinced he could heal him.

In the crush to see Jesus they dislodged roof tiles and lowered him into the house to get him close. Provocatively, Jesus said to the man something that only God could say: 'Your sins are forgiven.' When the Pharisees gasped, Jesus pointed out to them that saying four words is easy; healing someone is infinitely more difficult. He was implying that if he could prove his ability to work a miracle, they should readily accept his ability to forgive sins. Within minutes the paralysed man was walking, leaving the Pharisees with the awkward challenge that Jesus had offered a proof that he was God without using any words with which they could condemn him.

Not only did Jesus offer to forgive sins, he made other statements that were only for God to make. He called people to believe in him and to be loyal to him above any other – to acknowledge or reject him was to acknowledge or reject God. He invited people to come to him and rest – that way they would live eternally. He announced that whole countries would be judged by God on the basis of the way they treated him, expressed in the way they treated the world's poorest people.

With this kind of language, Jesus was pushing people to decide: these claims had to be stamped out or there had to be a radical rethink of Jewish beliefs. The Jewish leaders chose the former; the disciples chose the latter and became the founders of the movement that would be the Christian religion.

It was not an easy option for Jesus' friends, but there was no other way of making sense of what had happened to them. They began to do something unimaginable – to worship him.

want to know more?
- **Start by reading the Gospel of Mark, Paul's letter to the Philippians, and the first 60 psalms**
- *Jesus of Nazareth*, **Pope Benedict XVI, Bloomsbury, 2007**
- *The Jesus I Never Knew*, **Phillip Yancey, Zondervan, 2002**
- **www.rejesus.co.uk**

2 The Bible

A collection of documents written 2–3000 years
ago shapes the beliefs and practices of all
Christians. The texts recount the life of Jesus
and his first followers, tell the story of the
Jewish people in the centuries that preceded
him and include writings of many kinds about
what it means to be godly. They have been
studied, interpreted and wrestled with for
their changing relevance to each succeeding
generation. They are the scriptures of the
Christian people. This chapter explains how
the Bible is used (and sometimes abused)
to give Christians insight into God and the
purpose of life.

A book of books

There are at least 66 documents in the Bible. Of these, 39 were written before the time of Jesus, describing the history of the ancient Jewish people; 27 were written during the decades after Jesus, giving us an insight into his life and the teachings of the churches founded by his followers. Others are recognized as part of the Bible by some, but not all, Christians. Together they have shaped civilizations, both in the developed and developing worlds, more than any other book of the last 2000 years.

must know

Some definitions:
• **The canon is the collection of books that was established as belonging together because they were writings inspired by God as Scripture.**
• **The Septuagint is the translation of the Old Testament that was made from Hebrew to Greek by 70 scholars, sometimes nicknamed LXX.**
• **The Pentateuch comprises the first five books of the Bible, particularly revered in Judaism, where it is known as the Torah or the Law of Moses.**

The New Testament

The New Testament is the shorter of the two sections that make up the Bible. The documents in it ('books') were composed between 20 and 70 years after Jesus' resurrection. They were written mainly in Greek and copied by hand. During the second century collections were made which brought together the 27 which are now familiar, along with some others whose value was disputed. Time and study honoured those which, by the end of the fourth century, were formally recognized at a council of Christian leaders in Carthage (North Africa) as having an inherent authority allowing them to be trusted as inspired by God.

The books of the New Testament are:
• **The four gospels**, recounting the life of Jesus.
• **The Acts of the Apostles** ('Acts'), written by the author of Luke's gospel as a sequel.

This is a history covering the three decades after Jesus, telling the story of his followers.

- **Thirteen letters attributed to Paul**, the most dynamic missionary of the church's early years. Some were written to churches he had founded on the north coast of the Mediterranean Sea and beyond; others to church leaders.
- **Eight letters by other Christian leaders** ('epistles').
- **The Revelation to John** ('Revelation'), a collection of letters and visions, full of extravagant symbolism.

The Old Testament

The Old Testament, forming the first part of the Bible, is otherwise known as the Hebrew Scriptures. These writings are regarded as sacred by the Jewish religion, as well as by Christians. The documents were written in Hebrew between the fifth century and the second century BC, although parts of them probably existed in some form many years before and were brought together by editors.

Jesus knew and quoted them. However, the list of books that is regarded as inspired by God has never been so unambiguous as the New Testament. Two centuries before Jesus, the Hebrew Scriptures were translated into Greek. At that point, about 20 books that were not recognized as part of the canon were also translated. These are known as the Apocrypha, and appear in some Bibles but not in others. Some Christian groups regard these as inspired by God and part of their Scripture. Others regard them as helpful, but not as authoritative as the 66 books of the Old and New Testaments.

must know

- The Hebrews: the Jewish religion traces its roots to Abraham. He put his faith in God, who promised that his descendants through countless generations would receive his blessing. Abraham and his descendants through his son Isaac were known as the Hebrews.
- The Jews: ten centuries before Jesus, a civil war divided the Hebrew people into Israelites and Jews. The Israelites were overrun by a foreign enemy. The Jews, although enduring an exile, survived as a people. Resilient and faithful to God through repeated persecutions, today there are Jews worshipping in every continent.
- Israel: In the twentieth century, a secular state called Israel was established as a nation, controversially occupying territory which the Hebrews conquered in ancient times, and in which the Jews historically lived.

Different kinds of writing

The Bible does not set out a straightforward explanation of what it means to be a Christian. It is not a list of instructions from God. Instead it is a collection of many different kinds of prose and poetry. But Christians believe that, when it is read with faith and understanding, it reveals God to this generation in as vital a way as it did to its first readers.

must know

Although most Christians treat the myths of the Old Testament in the way they were originally intended, some use them to construct alternatives to mainstream scientific studies. Those who think in this 'literalist' way form a marginalized group in the developed world. However, a number of schools and museums (particularly in the USA) controversially present creation science as a fact, and deny that the world is as old as scientific understanding suggests.

Timeless stories

The Bible begins with timeless stories that were retold around the campfires of nomadic people for hundreds of years before they were written down. The technical name for these kinds of story is 'myths', meaning stories whose truth is so deep that conventional writing could not express it.

Through the story of a week of dazzling creativity, Genesis (the first book of the Bible) reveals that the existence of all matter from dust to DNA is not an accident, but has been brought about by an eternal and all-powerful God. Through the story of Adam and Eve disobeying God, it gives an explanation for why a world of beauty and joy is also a place where humans can find themselves suffering terribly at the hands of others. Through the story of Noah and his family escaping a great flood, it gives a reassurance that evil will not have the last word, but that the eternal destiny of those who trust God is secure.

Other parts of the Bible share the characteristics of these stories, making it difficult sometimes to distinguish history from myth.

History

The story of the Hebrew people is told in over a dozen of the Old Testament books, which overlap and bring together material from different sources. The history begins with Abraham. Abraham's belief (making him unique in his time) was that there was one sole God, and that he was invisible. God's call persuaded him to lead his household from their home in the region now known as Iraq, travel hundreds of miles, and settle in the land where Jesus would live many centuries later. In old age Abraham and his wife Sarah became parents of a boy named Isaac, a confirmation of God's promise that a vast nation of descendants would trace their ancestry to him.

Many years later, a famine sent the Hebrews to Egypt for their survival, where they were first welcomed, but subsequently oppressed and enslaved. Under the leadership of Moses they began to rediscover their identity as a worshipping community. They detected God's hand in a series of natural disasters that devastated the Egyptian economy. In a dramatic move that became known as the exodus, they defied their captors, crossed the Red Sea, and escaped into the desert beyond. It is this exodus (described in the book of the same name) that the Jewish people celebrate each year with Passover.

The Hebrews saw this release from slavery as the defining event that established them as a nation. Moses insisted that no tribal god was responsible for this. It had come about because the one true God whom Abraham had worshipped, Yahweh the Creator of all things, had willed it. God had done it

did you know?

Muslims also revere Abraham as a patriarch and the ancestor of Muhammad, founder of Islam. Before Isaac, Abraham fathered a boy named Ishmael, whose mother Hagar was one of his slaves. Muslims trace the ancestry of all Arab people to Abraham through Ishmael, while Jews trace their line through Isaac.

want to know more?

Where to find the stories of well-known Old Testament characters:
• Adam and Eve – Genesis 1-3.
• Noah's ark – Genesis 6-9.
• Abraham – Genesis 12-25.
• Joseph – Genesis 37-50.
• Moses – Exodus 1-40.
• Samson and Delilah – Judges 13-16.
• Ruth – Ruth 1-4.
• David – 1 Samuel 16-31 and 2 Samuel 1-24.
• Elijah – 1 Kings 17-21 and 2 Kings 1-2.
• Daniel – Daniel 1-6.
• Jonah – Jonah 1-4.

because, as a tiny, vulnerable people, they were the ideal vehicle through which to demonstrate his total superiority to all the world's superpowers and their worthless gods.

Four nomadic decades followed, during which the Hebrews were constantly reminded that with their great privilege came great responsibility. God had chosen them so that he could enrich the whole world through them. In the hardship of desert life, this was a concept they frequently resisted, being fractious and backward-looking. The focus of their worship was a large, ornate tent, the Tabernacle, in which they expressed devotion to God through the sacrifice of animals.

According to the accounts it was during these years that their legal system was established, spelling out what it meant to obey God and relate justly to others. The laws created standards for worship, and set proportional punishments for crime. They covered health, environmental concern, sexual propriety and an insistence that the most vulnerable (widows, orphans and refugees – unable to sustain themselves without work or family) should be protected. Among them were the Ten Commandments, which Christians also respect as their moral framework.

Moses was succeeded as the leader of the Hebrews by Joshua. Under him they focused their military capability and he led an invasion of Canaan, the land east of the Mediterranean which Abraham had made his home. A ferocious slaughter followed, after which the Hebrews took possession of what they described as their Promised Land. Their relationship with the surviving Canaanite people, and particularly their temptation in stressful times to turn to Canaanite gods for help, was a source of anguish for centuries. Under a series of religious and military leaders called judges, the people consolidated their domination of the territory.

It was, however, the foundation of a monarchy that was responsible for both their greatest triumph and their undoing. The Hebrews' most significant king was David who, about 1000 years before Jesus, united the tribes that had settled in different parts of the land and established Jerusalem as his capital city, economically and militarily secure. David, typically of all the Old Testament heroes, is portrayed as both flawed and godly. His son Solomon was responsible for building the first temple to Yahweh on Mount Zion in Jerusalem.

Solomon's successor, however, occupied his throne in a tyrannical way, prompting a civil war which divided those who lived in the northern territories (the Israelites) from those in the south (the Jews). Israel was conquered by Assyria, and its dispersed inhabitants never again had a national identity. Judah, the southern kingdom, endured for over a century before it too was overrun.

Most of the defeated Jews were taken as captives to Babylon. They were brutalized and utterly demoralized in the belief that they had lost not only their homeland but also, in the rubble of the temple, their God. Their exile, however, proved to be a time during which it was possible for them to prosper. They became aware that God had not only come with them to Babylon, but was everywhere. Worship in local synagogues began. The Scriptures were collected. And it was during those years that the

must know

Moses had a mystical encounter with God in the desert. In front of a blazing bush, God revealed his name to be Yahweh. It means 'I am who I am' (and always have been and always will be). This name for God became extremely precious to the Hebrews – a token of their unique relationship with him. In English Bibles it is sometimes given as Jehovah or the LORD (using capital letters).

expectation of a future Messiah developed. After seven decades they began to be repatriated. The last historical narratives of the Old Testament describe the Jews returning to the Promised Land led by Ezra, Nehemiah and Zerubbabel.

During the four centuries that passed before the New Testament resumes the story, the Jews became subjects of different superpowers, including Alexander the Great's Greek empire, the Ptolemies and the Selucids. For a century there was Jewish independence, following an uprising led by Judas Maccabaeus. But about 60 years before Jesus was born, Judas' descendants were locked in a power struggle and the side with the upper hand made a treaty ceding control to the rapidly expanding Roman empire. The emperor in Rome appointed a puppet 'king of the Jews', Herod the Great (the one who was so disturbed to learn of someone who might have a rival claim to that title – Jesus).

Prophecy

Prophets were (and are) people called to speak for God to his people. Between the fifth and ninth centuries before Jesus, some of them had their words recorded in seventeen books collected in the Old Testament. Their message was sometimes written, sometimes spoken and sometimes acted out dramatically.

The popular view of a prophet is of someone who can predict the future, but in fact the Old Testament prophets almost invariably had an insight into the present. They called God's people to bring to mind the journey on which God had faithfully led them and analyzed the shortcomings of their current relationship with him. It is because they anticipated the consequences of the Jews and Israelites failing to reform

their ways and return to God that they had a reputation
for foresight.

The message of the prophets was that Yahweh the
Lord presides over all history, and that despite the worst
excesses of humans and their leaders, a just and holy
ruler is ultimately in control. The response of men and
women should not be to forge international alliances,
which would involve compromise when it came to
acknowledging their gods, but to put themselves
exclusively on the side of Yahweh – a fact that the
prophets restate again and again, sometimes in anger,

Some Old Testament prophets, in their own words

• Hosea: 'Hear the word of the LORD, you Israelites ...
There is no faithfulness, no love, no acknowledgment of God in the land.
There is only cursing, lying and murder, stealing and adultery...
Because of this the land mourns, and all who live in it waste away.' (4:1–3)
• Jeremiah: 'The time is coming,' declares the LORD, 'when I will make a new
covenant with the house of Israel and with the house of Judah ...
I will be their God, and they will be my people ...
For I will forgive their wickedness and will remember their sins no more.'
(31:31–34)
• Isaiah: 'The people walking in darkness have seen a great light;
on those living in the land of the shadow of death a light has dawned ...
For to us a child is born, to us a son is given,
and the government will be on his shoulders.
And he will be called Wonderful Counsellor, Mighty God,
Everlasting Father, Prince of Peace.
Of the increase of his government and peace there will be no end.
He will reign on David's throne and over his kingdom,
establishing and upholding it with justice and righteousness
from that time on and forever.' (9:2,6,7)

sometimes in tenderness. Their strongest accusation was that the people of God had forsaken their obligations to seek justice for the poorest among them – their impeccable displays of worship were rendered meaningless because the most vulnerable members of society were being exploited. The prophets believed that calamity was inevitable for the nation, and that when it happened it would be a sign of God's judgement. Through all their writing, though, runs a thread of hope that God would be the people's saviour and this hope came to be expressed most clearly in the anticipation of the Messiah.

Songs and wise sayings

Large sections of the Old Testament are poetry. The 150 psalms that make up the book of that name formed a cycle of songs for use in temple worship. They find room for virtually every sentiment humans need to express to God – praise, doubt, pleading, trust, recollection of good times, and despair in bad times.

The problem of whether it is possible to believe in an all-loving God when suffering is so prevalent in the world is the subject of Job, presented as a verse drama. The possibility that food, drink, sun and sex are all you need to get through life is discussed with surprising sympathy in Ecclesiastes. And Proverbs collects the sayings of the wise men and women of Israel, using riddles, jokes and maxims to advise on a godly attitude to work, shopping, money, health and friendship.

The poetry and wisdom of the Old Testament

● Words of praise, crediting to God the joy of being alive:
'I waited patiently for the LORD; he turned to me and heard my cry.
He lifted me out of the slimy pit, out of the mud and mire;
he set my feet on a rock and gave me a firm place to stand.
He put a new song in my mouth, a hymn of praise to our God.
Many will see and fear and put their trust in the LORD.'
(Psalm 40:1-3)

● Torment that God does not intervene to end suffering:
'I cry out to you, O God, but you do not answer;
I stand up, but you merely look at me.
Have I not wept for those in trouble? Has not my soul grieved for the poor?
Yet when I hoped for good, evil came;
when I looked for light, then came darkness.' (Job 30:20,25,26)

● Erotic tenderness:
'Let him kiss me with the kisses of his mouth –
for your love is more delightful than wine.
Pleasing is the fragrance of your perfumes;
your name is like perfume poured out.
No wonder the maidens love you!
Take me away with you – let us hurry!
Let the king bring me into his chambers.' (Song of Songs 1:2-4)

● Proverbial advice for leading a godly life:
'Do not gaze at wine when it is red,
when it sparkles in the cup, when it goes down smoothly!
In the end it bites like a snake and poisons like a viper.
Your eyes will see strange sights
and your mind imagine confusing things.' (Proverbs 23:31-33)

Gospels

The New Testament begins with four accounts of Jesus' life. Not much was written about him for 30 years after his resurrection, because the eyewitnesses were mainly illiterate and the culture involved stories being passed on by word of mouth. The expectation was that the promised return of Jesus to earth was imminent, so making a written record was not regarded as a priority until a new generation of children who had not met Jesus matured.

Mark, beginning to write his gospel in about 65, filled it with action and raced through Jesus' life. Matthew, writing ten to 20 years later, based his account on Mark's. He copied some parts word for word, and expanded it to explain how Jesus fulfilled all that the Old Testament anticipated. Luke approached his task as a teacher, also starting with Mark's account and enlarging it to stress the salvation that Jesus had brought. There are some stories that appear both in Matthew and Luke, but not in Mark, so academics suggest that they both knew an anthology of Jesus' sayings that has now been lost (called 'The Source' and nicknamed 'Q'). Because of their similiarity, these three are known as 'the synoptic gospels' (meaning that they see eye-to-eye). Like the rest of the New Testament, they were written in Greek.

John's gospel, written rather later, is different. He went further in explaining how Jesus' teaching revealed God. He did not try to be comprehensive in his account of Jesus' life, but highlighted particular events with commentaries that made clear their significance.

The author of Luke's gospel went on to write a sequel, the Acts of the Apostles, which describes the expansion of the Christian church. In it, he focuses first on the remaining disciples, reinvigorated by God's Spirit after Jesus' departure. Peter leads a growing church in Jerusalem, but the followers of Jesus are scattered during a time of persecution and plant new churches wherever they go. Paul subsequently takes centre stage, becoming Christianity's first great missionary, and the story climaxes with him preaching boldly in Rome at the very heart of the known world.

Letters

Most of the 21 letters collected in the New Testament were written before the gospels were completed. More than half of them carry Paul's signature. Although he never met Jesus in person, Paul had a vision of him while on a journey from Jerusalem to Damascus. Ironically, at the time he was on a mission to arrest the followers of Jesus who had left Jerusalem when it became too dangerous for them to stay there. The drama of an encounter with the heavenly Jesus was such that he became convinced that Jesus was the Messiah, a fact confirmed to him by retreating to present-day Turkey to spend several years studying the Hebrew Scriptures in the light of his experience.

Paul might have stayed there researching had not an unexpected development taken place. Although the men and women committed to the way of Jesus had initially been exclusively Jewish, scattering from Jerusalem they could not stop themselves talking about what they had discovered. In some places, non-Jews were joining the movement. Having changed his own beliefs so comprehensively, Paul was seen as the ideal person to help with the colossal change that would be involved in incorporating these Gentiles into the new Christian sect.

Brought to Antioch, Paul prepared the church for international mission. It expressed itself first in a practical

Paul's letters to the Corinthians

The new churches to which Paul wrote were fragile. The congregation in Corinth probably numbered only about 50, but they were already in danger of splitting into two rival groups. Paul addressed at least two letters to them, focusing their attention on the resurrection of Jesus, teaching them how to worship, and pleading with them to unite. They include some of the most inspirational words in the Bible:

- 'If I give all I possess to the poor and surrender my body to the flames, but have not love, I gain nothing. Love is patient, love is kind. It does not envy, it does not boast, it is not proud. It is not rude, it is not self-seeking, it is not easily angered, it keeps no record of wrongs. Love does not delight in evil but rejoices with the truth. It always protects, always trusts, always hopes, always perseveres. Love never fails.'

(1 Corinthians 13:3-8)

- 'God, who said, "Let light shine out of darkness," made his light shine in our hearts to give us the light of the knowledge of the glory of God in the face of Christ. But we have this treasure in jars of clay to show that this all-surpassing power is from God and not from us. We are hard pressed on every side, but not crushed; perplexed, but not in despair; persecuted, but not abandoned; struck down, but not destroyed.'

(2 Corinthians 4:6-9)

response to a famine many miles south in Jerusalem, and then in a series of journeys taking the good news of Jesus further and further afield, founding Christian communities in major towns when both Jews and Gentiles responded to their message.

Most of Paul's letters were written to the churches he had founded. These fledgling churches were small and vulnerable, and in response Paul was an encouraging and challenging writer. He made clear issues of doctrine, explaining why Jesus' death and resurrection have a significance not just on a human scale, but in cosmic terms. He set out what it means for God to have reconciled himself to the world through what Jesus did. He also went into detail about what the ethical response of Christians should be to God's blessing. Particular issues in each church led him to spell out what was appropriate behaviour in that context.

Most of the other letters in the New Testament had a less specific original audience and were written to scattered groups of Christians. They urged God's people to have faith, even if it meant suffering persecution as a result. They were full of practical advice for godly living. Some address misconceptions about the true nature of Jesus. All of them show God reaching out in abundant love to humankind.

The final book of the Bible, Revelation, also begins with letters to churches. They use heightened and poetic language, though, describing the strengths and weaknesses of the congregations as they face persecution from outside and wayward beliefs or apathy inside. The book goes on to recount flamboyant visions of beasts and angels. Written in a kind of code, this allowed the persecuted church of the first century to recognize contemporary world events and take hope that evil would not prevail. Generations of subsequent Christians, although often baffled, have rejoiced that it points forward to the ultimate triumph of God and an eternity of justice and peace in his presence.

Study and interpretation

More than any other document, the Bible has been scrutinized by academics and enquirers. Its stories are the last thing some children hear before they sleep and its writings the first thing some Christians read when they wake. In their different ways, each of them is wanting the Bible to offer up its truth.

Studying the Bible

In order to benefit most fully from the Bible, the Christian church has encouraged a method of reading it that holds two approaches in tension – a thorough, academic analysis of the Bible, and an openness to receive it as a means through which God actively communicates with this generation.

The first approach requires the Bible to be analyzed like any other historic document of the same age and importance. For the most part, the Christian church has welcomed a critical study of their Scriptures by theologians. Those who have the expertise to put the texts in the context of the world in which they were written – its culture, its politics, and other literature of the time – reveal insights that are not obvious on the surface.

The process of drawing out the original meaning of the text is known as 'exegesis'. When it is undertaken as an academic study, it involves, among other things:

• scrutinizing the shades of meaning that particular Greek or Hebrew words would have had at the time they were written

• considering what happened to the stories of Jesus and the narratives of the Old Testament during the years when they were passed on by word of mouth

- researching what history and archaeology can reveal about the places and events described in the text
- analyzing how the writers of the books selected and shaped the material, including or omitting details
- identifying the date and location of composition.

Books that draw together this information are known as commentaries, and they usually examine the text verse by verse. These books are valuable, because they clean away the varnish that passing time and changing culture paints over the Bible's original intentions. Meanings that have been distorted or obscured become clear again.

Their drawback is that the theologian who writes the commentary brings his or her own presuppositions to it. For example, some hold the view that church leaders in the decades after Jesus challenged or encouraged their congregations by inventing stirring phrases or incidents and attributing them to Jesus. Others begin with the assumption that Jesus' sayings were so significant to the original witnesses that they preserved them carefully. So words of Jesus that are prescient about the suffering that would overtake Jerusalem are seen in some commentaries as far-sighted warnings, and in others as attributed retrospectively to him by those who were living through it.

Interpreting the Bible

The second approach recognizes that there is a sense in which the Bible can seize the imagination of believers and become one of the ways they find themselves in touch with the will and ways of God. For those who make a decision to place themselves under its authority the Bible is an inspired book, through which God is still communicating in a potent way.

must know

Testament means covenant or deal. So the Old Testament refers to the old deal that God made with the Jewish people ('You will be my people and I will be your God'). This covenant was expressed in the blessing of God, and the provision of a homeland (their Promised Land) in the territory now shared by Palestine and Israel. The Jews were to respond with uncompromised devotion and obedience.

The New Testament refers to the new deal that God made with humankind in the person of Jesus. This covenant, priceless because only the death and resurrection of Jesus could achieve it, reconciles God and humans for all eternity. Every requirement of the contract has been undertaken by God, leaving humans with nothing to do – other than accept God's grace.

In the eighteenth century the fact that the New Testament accepted slavery as a way of life led some Christians to support it in the belief that God had ordained it. It was an increasing understanding of the Bible's status as a book written in and for a particular culture that led Christian leaders to reconsider this. Centuries of Christian tradition had expanded understanding of what it means for all humans to be equal. Seeing slavery in that context changed their discernment of God's will so thoroughly that (although it took many years) eventually all the world's Christian communities condemned slavery as an evil.

The same desire to honour the authority of the Bible, but also to recognize that God's intention for the world progresses alongside human development, prompts heated discussions within the church today about homosexuality.

This involves a technique of interpretation known as hermeneutics, which means discerning what God is saying through the Bible to the world, a community or individual today. Most Christians engage with the Bible in a devotional way, either by reading it themselves or by attending public worship at which the Bible is interpreted in sermons or discussions. It is through an intelligent and open-minded engagement with the Scriptures that Christians edge toward an understanding of the mind of God on matters that are directly relevant to their lives or societies.

This approach to the Bible also has potential drawbacks. An attempt to take concepts that are 2000 years old and direct them thoughtlessly at the very different culture of the twenty-first century (that is, without having done exegesis first in order to understand their significance) can generate ideas that are at best eccentric and at worst damaging.

Appreciating the Bible

Read in the English translation made in the seventeenth century, the Bible is majestically beautiful but not easy to understand. Research during the last 50 years has allowed for translations that are either more accurate for study or more accessible for devotional reading, although rarely both together.

Study uncovers a book that is profound and fascinating, but leaves people with questions about its apparent contradictions and its complex picture of God. Neither objective nor scientific, it speaks the language of faith.

Devotional reading reveals a book that is inspirational and life-changing, but not straightforward. It offers spiritual insights that harmonize so completely with human experience that it seems to lay bare life's meaning. It can disturb, but its over-arching message that there is a purpose to existence because of a good and loving God is exhilarating. Even Christians who struggle to rise to its intellectual challenges attest that reading the Bible improves their lives.

However, the Bible needs to be read in a context that recognizes that its words are not magical messages from God. It describes itself as literature that is inspired by God, but communicated through the thought and style of an author. Describing the Old Testament (but equally true of the New Testament) the writer of Peter's letters suggests: 'Prophets, though human, spoke from God as they were carried along by the Holy Spirit.'

want to know more?

• *Introducing the New Testament*, John Drane, Lion Hudson, 1999
• *Introducing the Old Testament*, John Drane, Lion Hudson, 2000
• *How to Read the Bible for All Its Worth*, Gordon Fee and Douglas Stuart, Scripture Union, 1994
• www.biblegateway.com

3 What Christians believe

Over 2000 years, the message of Jesus has
been open to interpretation in a million ways.
The result is that those who seek to follow
him describe their beliefs in different ways.
However, all Christians believe three
straightforward things. Firstly, there is a God.
Secondly, in a way so unique that it is beyond
human understanding, God touched this
planet 2000 years ago in the person of Jesus.
And thirdly, that matters! In this chapter you
will read about the simplicity of those ideas,
but also explore the complexity of the varied
ways in which Christians have sought to
understand them.

There is a God

At some point in their life every human being asks him- or herself what the purpose of being alive is. The question may arise when a person is confronted by a death, or contemplating a new life, or wondering whether change is possible. For a Christian, the answer to that question is shaped by the belief that something bigger, wiser and older than any object in the cosmos is responsible for its existence. And that something can be known – it could, in fact, be described as someone. There is a God.

The nature of life

It may be that life has developed over time in a way that was not driven by any particular purpose, and it is by chance that humans have such a rich range of skills and emotions. Most life on the planet seems content just to exist – lichen on a rock, for instance. Science has offered a possible explanation of life in which there is a line between those simple forms and the complex nature of humanity.

In contrast, Christians believe that the progression which leads from a particle of matter to a human being has been brought about by a living God who has always existed independently of any entity. The diversity and order, the beauty and interdependence of the natural world points to the activity of a creator God, rather than to undirected processes in which the fittest flourish. A song recorded among the Old Testament psalms puts it: 'The heavens declare the glory of God; the skies

must know

Contrasting views of whether examining the world leads to belief in a purposeful God:
• 'Life exists in the universe only because the carbon atom possesses certain exceptional properties ... Life may be a disease which attacks planets in their decay.' (Sir James Jeans, twentieth-century cosmologist).
• 'The God who made the world and everything in it is the Lord of heaven and earth and does not live in temples built by hands. And he is not served by human hands, as if he needed anything, because he himself gives all life and breath and everything else.' (Paul, recorded in Acts 17:24,25)

proclaim the work of his hands.' If this is true then humans, the most complex elements of the creation, have been brought to their enviable state of existence for a reason, and the key to finding that reason is to acknowledge the maker of all things, who must be powerful, clever and praiseworthy beyond compare.

What kind of God?

Christians believe that God has revealed himself not just in the creation that they can see, but in greater detail through the Bible, through people's experience and, most directly of all, through Jesus. The God revealed in this way is both transcendent (meaning that he has an existence beyond time, beyond space, beyond anything that the human mind can imagine) and also immanent (meaning that he is closely involved with the universe and able to relate personally to people).

The Christian God is not one who has called the creation into existence and then abandoned it to run itself, nor is he so domineering that every turn of a page happens because he wills it. He is ultimately in control of all that he has created, but within that his creation (including every human) has freedom. The result is both pattern and unpredictability. God is achieving his purpose, which is described in the New Testament as bringing together all things – heavenly and earthly, created and divine – into an eternity of perfection. And to do so, he has set his loving concern upon this earth and its inhabitants (an aspect of God that requires great faith from men and women now that the scale by which the universe dwarfs them is clear).

must know

Not only is God above space and time, he is also above language and gender. This causes problems whenever God is referred to in writing, because neither 'he' (which this book uses) nor 'she' can possibly do justice to the nature of God's being. The Bible frequently employs the word Father in association with God, and occasionally uses metaphors that imply Motherhood. In Judaism the Old Testament name of God, Yahweh, is revered as so holy that it is never spoken aloud – not only beyond gender, but beyond utterance.

must know

Over the centuries, theologians (people who academically or informally try to understand God) have attempted to prove the existence of God. Anselm in the eleventh century and Thomas Aquinas in the thirteenth century set out so-called proofs. They have continued to be intriguing, but it is faith, not proof, that leads Christians toward their God:
• The cosmological argument suggests that everything that happens is caused by something, so a chain of events must lead back to a First Cause that set all else going.
• The teleological argument declares that the design and purpose evident in the world inevitably points to a Designer.
• The ontological argument is a complex piece of philosophical logic conjecturing that God, greater than anything else that can be conceived, must exist or he would not be the greatest conceivable being.
• The moral argument suggests that our sense of right and wrong must come from a just Creator, because the dust from which we come has no morality of its own.

There are some aspects of God's being that are completely unique to him:
• **God is everywhere** (the technical term is 'omnipresent'). He does not live in a place that is apart from his creation, but is present everywhere in it, not only in its physicality, but also morally and spiritually.
• **God is absolutely powerful** (omnipotent). Evil things happen in the context of a God who can and will deliver justice.
• **God knows everything** (omniscient). When prayer is offered, it is made to a God who understands all things, spoken and secret, and knows the end from the beginning.
• **God is beyond space and time.** Unlike the changing and decaying world he is eternal and dependent on no one for his existence.
• **God is good.** At the heart of the universe, no matter what malice or suffering appears to have the upper hand, is goodness.
• **God is holy.** Holiness is all that sets God's being apart from that of humans. His purity and perfection ought to make him unapproachably awesome.
• **God is love.** God's holiness would be unbearable, were it not for the fact that the Bible also sums up the entire nature of God as love. This aspect of God brings him so close to humans that being indwelt by God is an entirely positive experience. God's love expresses itself in faithfulness, forgiveness and blessing (although not in the removal of all hardship).

In the second century Irenaeus, a bishop in present-day France, wrote: 'In the beginning,

God fashioned [humankind] not because he had any need of them, but in order that he might have creatures on whom to bestow his love.' For Christians, knowing that the God who is almighty also has an intense and personal love for them is both uplifting and consoling.

Three in one

The Bible gives Christians a problem to solve when it describes God. It speaks of God as the Father, creator of all things. It also speaks of Jesus as God, and it speaks of God as Spirit, present and active in the world and in humans (the Holy Spirit, known in former times as the Holy Ghost).

However, the Bible never suggests that Christians have three Gods. Rather, it always insists that there is one God. Over the first Christian centuries, theologians laboured to reconcile these facts without diminishing the integrity of any part of the Bible. Through councils and creeds they forged the doctrine that there is one God, who exists in three distinct identities – God the Father, God the Son and God the Holy Spirit.

When God is referred to as three in one, the word used is Trinity. Each member is referred to as God in the New Testament, but it also distinguishes between them and their roles. God is a God in community. In reflection of that, Christianity is a community religion – believers are made one with the community that is God, and become part of the community that is the church.

The three sections of this chapter reflect those three personalities of God, distinct, but equal and united.

must know

Among the many references in the Bible to the God who is three in one are these:
- 'Jesus came and preached peace to you who were far away and peace to those who were near. For through the Son all have access to the Father by one Spirit.' (Ephesians 2:17,18)
- 'I keep asking that the God of our Lord Jesus Christ, the glorious Father, may give you the Spirit of wisdom and revelation, so that you may know him better.' (Ephesians 1:17)

In the image of God

Humans did not create God; God created humans. Unique among all living things, there are ways in which human beings share God's nature (they are 'in his image'). They have a moral sense, they are intellectual and creative, they have a spirituality, they share the responsibility for the earth's conservation, and death will not be the end for them because they were made to be with God eternally.

However, in a vital way, humans are not like the perfect God. Made with the freedom to choose, men and women have chosen sin. Individually people do wrong things; corporately our world organizes itself in an unjust way. So pervasive is wrongdoing in the world that the Bible sees it as an overwhelming condition. Humanity has deliberately rejected the ways of God and become separated from him. 'The fall', as it is known, has plunged humans into a tragic condition. Men and women do not have the ability to rescue themselves and reunite with God. Only God can take that initiative.

Angels and demons

Some strands of Christian belief emphasize references in the Bible to angels – spiritual beings that are neither God nor human, but have existed alongside the Trinity, worshipping and doing God's will from the beginning. In art and literature, obscure references in the Bible have been filled out to suggest that one of them, Satan, rebelled against God, was expelled from his presence, and became the agent of all evil. Other Christian traditions do not require a devil figure to account for wrongdoing in humans, and see accounts of angels and demons as metaphors for spiritual activity.

God has touched this planet

No one seriously doubts that Jesus was a historical figure. But what was his nature? And what was it about his life and death that leads Christians to believe that the relationship between God and humankind is changed irrevocably?

Who was Jesus?

During his lifetime, there was discussion and rumour about who Jesus was. The four men who wrote the gospels, though, were convinced that he had uniquely crossed the line that separates humans from their creator. During the early Christian centuries several views of Jesus' nature were put forward by those who wanted to understand what had happened during his 30 extraordinary years. It is the final one that emerged over time as the mainstream belief of Christian people:

• **Was Jesus merely a human?** Jews of Jesus' day would have known other miracle-workers who met tragic ends. Esteemed in life as imposing people, they were largely forgotten as disappointments once buried. Historical scholarship today also tends to be sceptical about the New Testament's suggestions of Jesus' divinity, stressing instead his moral leadership.

• **Was Jesus a human whom God exalted?** In the excitable nationalistic fervour of Jesus' time, there was an eagerness among Jews to identify Jesus as the Messiah. Like Abraham, Moses and David before him, this would have meant Jesus was regarded as a human so special that God 'adopted' and anointed him. For several centuries groups of Christians remained Jewish and revered Jesus as their Messiah. A small movement of 'Messianic Jews' re-emerged in the twentieth century.

must know

A example of the writing of gnostic groups is the Gospel of Thomas, with its 'secret sayings of Jesus'. There was, however, never a point at which it was considered authentic enough to be included in the New Testament. By the fourth century Christian leaders were warning people not to read what they considered fabricated documents being passed off as eyewitness accounts.

A hymn written very soon after Jesus' life, which Paul quoted in one of his letters, describes Jesus as fully human and fully God:
- **'Jesus, being in very nature God,**
did not consider equality with God something to be grasped,
but made himself nothing,
taking the very nature of a servant,
being made in human likeness.
And being found in appearance as a human being,
he humbled himself and became obedient to death – even death on a cross!
Therefore God exalted him to the highest place
and gave him the name that is above every name,
that at the name of Jesus every knee should bow,
in heaven and on earth and under the earth,
and every tongue confess that Jesus Christ is Lord,
to the glory of God the Father.' (Philippians 2:6-11)

● **Was Jesus a god sent so that others could become divine?** The culture of the Roman empire in which Jesus lived was dominated by the legacy of the ancient Greeks (usually called 'Hellenistic' culture). For them, the boundaries between divine and human were not definite (Greek gods often disguised themselves as human beings). Influenced by this, some groups in the years after Jesus declared that he had special wisdom ('gnosis') that could unlock the sacred potential of their lives. These 'gnostic' groups who believed that Jesus could make them divine were ruled to have eccentric beliefs and their writings were suppressed. Today, however, there are New Age groups seeking to help people 'get in touch with the god within them'.

● **Was Jesus fully God as well as fully human?** The view that dominates the New Testament, and particularly the writings of Paul, is that Jesus had an intrinsic connection with God. He was, like no one before or since, fully God but also fully a man. This is the view that has dominated Christian thought since shortly after Jesus' life. Jesus was with God at the very beginning of all things; he will be with God at the close of the human era. For a brief moment in eternal terms, Jesus inhabited a human body - he was born, grew and died as a man. But having the nature of God, death was not the end of him. Unlike a gnostic version of Christianity, men and women are not saved by looking in, but by looking up to Jesus 'the Lord'. They are not changed into gods, but into beings in whom Jesus is living. That transformation can begin in the earthly body of a Christian, but it will endure beyond death and culminate in a resurrection to eternal life in God's presence.

The Saviour

There is within all men and women a spiritual element that leads them to reach out for something beyond bare physical existence. The search for something transcendent is addressed in various ways – for instance, music, drugs and sex have played a part in virtually every culture as humans seek experiences that expand both the meaning and the mystery of life. Christians recognize this yearning, and explain it as a need for salvation.

The Bible describes in different ways what it is that we need to be saved from – meaninglessness, suffering, oppression, self. For Paul, the key needs were for salvation from death and from sin. In his theology they were combined because he described sin as a kind of death. (He had in mind not the watered-down and sexualized definition of sin in popular usage today, but the cold, greedy and meaningless sin that grips individuals and nations and is deathly.) The heart of Christian belief is that the life, death and resurrection of Jesus can release people from this.

Christianity has developed several metaphors to explain what it is about Jesus that created the circumstances in which salvation can take place. They are called 'theories of atonement' (atonement meaning being reconciled 'at one' with God):

• **A substitution.** This way of understanding Jesus' significance begins with the belief that all sin must be punished, since God has justice at the heart of his nature. Because all humans have sinned, all must be punished by a death that excludes them from God's presence. However, Jesus (himself sinless) becomes a substitute for humankind. On the cross, he willingly accepts the punishment that humans deserve. He suffers death instead of us, meaning that God's need to see justice

must know

The understanding of Jesus' death as a substitute for humans, punished by an angry God, is known as 'penal substitution' or 'substitutionary atonement'. It has unexpectedly become contentious in recent years. Bitter words have been spoken against some Christian leaders who suggest that its picture of a bloodthirsty God is unhelpful. It is the favoured explanation of salvation in the sections of the Western church where most new hymns are written, which means that lyrics expressing it are sung so widely that many Christians assume it to be the only explanation.

This is how the gospel of John describes why Jesus (the Son of Man) was lifted to his death on a cross:
'The Son of Man must be lifted up, that everyone who believes in him may have eternal life. For God so loved the world that he gave his one and only Son, that whoever believes in him shall not perish but have eternal life. For God did not send his Son into the world to condemn the world, but to save the world through him.'
(John 3:14-17)

done has been addressed, and nothing can now keep humans from his love.

● **An identification.** It is also possible to see Jesus' death as the most extreme expression of God's willingness to cross the divide between himself and humankind. Out of his immense love, God chooses to share humanity's worst experience, and allows himself to be hated, to experience pain and to die. He makes himself at one with humanity at its worst, creating the circumstances in which they can be at one with him in heaven's best.

● **A victory.** The earliest artistic representations of Jesus do not show him on the cross, but in the triumph that followed his resurrection. The pre-eminent picture of Jesus was as a victor over all that is evil. When Jesus died on the cross, evil made its strongest bid to defeat God. When Jesus rose from the dead, God conquered evil, which can no longer keep humans from him.

No one theory has ever been adopted by the church as the official view of something that is clearly beyond human comprehension. Other metaphors that have helped Christians edge toward an understanding are variations on them. Among them are:

● **Jesus the ransom**, paid to Satan as the price for liberating humans from slavery, with sin as their master;

● **Jesus the sacrifice**, that put an end to the need for animal sacrifices, because he was perfect and God could forgive without any more blood being shed;

● **Jesus the supreme example**, who by allowing self-giving love to overcome everything negative, inspires humankind to a transformation that could not be attained without him.

In each case, trying to understand how Jesus has changed the relationship between humans and God leads back to a man dying on a cross. This is why the cross has become the central symbol of Christianity.

The cross sums up the depths to which humans can sink. But it also reveals the full extent of God's love. Although Jesus could effortlessly have summoned divine power in order to dominate the world, he chose instead to submit to evil. Love showed itself to be more compelling than power.

Christians frequently dwell on the irony that it was at the moment of the world's greatest wickedness that the greatest love was revealed. Exploring this at a personal level leads to a point at which they can say with heartfelt gratitude, 'Jesus died for me'. People often see in themselves some of the instincts that have made a world in which it was inevitable that someone as good as Jesus would meet a terrible end. That recognition of a need for forgiveness and change – humanly unattainable – is the moment at which the full extent of Jesus' love is made clear. The cross that shows the extent of sin shows the extent of salvation. Because of it, God has dealt with everything that might hinder people receiving the unreserved welcome of his friendship.

When they dwell on the significance of the cross at a global level, Christians glimpse the possibility that there might be a reason why God's beautiful world is also a place of suffering. Jesus' humiliation and murder shows that God is not remote or uncaring about people's anguish; he is intimately involved in the pain of it. This does not explain why God chooses not to take pain away (for which no answer seems satisfactory). However, the crucifixion shows us a God who suffers alongside his creation, agonized and heartbroken, at one with the people he loves. Though not an explanation, it is a profound consolation.

must know

A belief unique to Roman Catholics is that there is an indeterminate state between this world and Heaven known as Purgatory. Although not found in the Bible, the concept emerged in the early centuries of Christianity. It is a place where the souls of humans can be purified and made ready for Heaven. Although not a state of eternal punishment, it is a joyless place where justice is meted out for earthly wrongdoing. It can be shortened by the prayers of those remaining on earth, speeding a person's passage to Heaven. During the upheaval that took place in the sixteenth-century church this concept was rejected, and it does not feature in churches that have been founded since then.

It matters!

If the creation of the world and the life of Jesus were events locked in history, both could be ignored. However, the experience of Christians is that God is alive and active in the world through the Holy Spirit.

It matters in death

Christians are realistic about death and its sadness, but they believe that death is not the end. A Christian funeral service encourages people to grieve (which Jesus himself did), but this happens in the context of hope, sometimes even joy. It asserts that, beyond death, people will meet God. Meeting God can seem like the fulfilment of a life's eager ambition, or it can seem like a terrifying prospect. There is good news!

The good news is, however, not escapist. Central to the nature of God is his justice and Christians believe that everyone will be required to account for their actions and failures. In particular it will be their behaviour toward those who are poor or suffering that will be made plain in God's presence. Obviously this experience will be very different for those who have been oppressors, those who have been apathetic, and those who have been sinned against.

Christians are able to contemplate meeting God on this Day of Justice (sometimes called the Day of Judgement) with absolute confidence that it will be a positive experience, and will usher in peace and gladness. This is not because they will be proved to have done more good than harm (which no one can claim with certainty). Rather, it is because God is absolutely loving even in circumstances where that love is undeserved. The result of Jesus' actions is that repentance and faith are met with forgiveness and unrestrained welcome.

Heaven and Hell

The Bible speaks of Heaven as a reality, but its nature is only hinted at. The most clear statements are about what will cease once and for all – pain, tears and death itself. Further suggestions are given in picture form – a hospitable place of food and friendship; an exhilarating place of music and beauty. Essential to it all is the lively and magnificent presence of God. There is no suggestion at all of reincarnation in Christian belief. Rather there is an assurance that in heaven men, women and children, completely healed and with their identity enriched to its full potential, will enjoy each other and enjoy God in a context of love.

The Bible also speaks of Hell, but it is more difficult to identify its nature. At the time of Jesus there was a garbage dump outside Jerusalem called Gehenna, on which fires burned and people in abject poverty picked over the remains to find scraps. A place of extreme wretchedness, it was despised as having once been a site of pagan child sacrifice. Jesus threatened that those who sinned would end up there. He obviously cannot have meant this literally. However, this did not stop church leaders of the Middle Ages onwards painting vivid pictures (in words from a pulpit; in paint on church walls) of a judgement after death in which faithful churchgoers were lifted to joy with the angels and the wicked pitchforked into fire with the devils. Theologians today are more likely to consider how separation from God, once the fullness of his purpose for creation has been revealed, would involve spiritual misery comparable with the terrible place at which Jesus was looking when he used the word Hell.

A 'universalist' view of Heaven suggests that Jesus' death and resurrection took place for the whole of humankind. Because God's love has triumphed, everyone without exception will be welcomed into his presence. Other Christians maintain that acceptance into heaven is

must know

Words of assurance written by Paul:
• 'Christ Jesus, who died – more than that, who was raised to life – is at the right hand of God and is also interceding for us … I am convinced that neither death nor life, neither angels nor demons, neither the present nor the future, nor any powers, neither height nor depth, nor anything else in all creation, will be able to separate us from the love of God that is in Christ Jesus our Lord.' (Romans 8:34,38,39)

must know

'God has created me to do some definite service; he has committed some work to me which he has not committed to another. I have my mission – I may never know it in this life, but I shall be told it in the next.

'I am a link in a chain, a bond of connection between persons. He has not created me for naught. I shall do good. I shall do his work. I shall be an angel of peace, a preacher of truth in my own place while not intending it, if I do but keep his commandments. Therefore I will trust him.

'Whatever, wherever I am, I can never be thrown away. If I am in sickness, my sickness may serve him; in perplexity, my perplexity may serve him; in sorrow, my sorrow may serve him. He does nothing in vain. He knows what he is about.

'He may take away my friends. He may throw me among strangers. He may make me feel desolate, make my spirit sink, hide my future from me – still he knows what he is about.'
John Henry Newman

conditional on a decision being made to follow Jesus during life. Those who have rejected him during their lives will be excluded from Heaven and either cease to exist or suffer the punishment of eternal regret.

These things are unknowable. However, Christians can face their death and that of those they love in complete confidence of two things. God is supremely just and it is inconceivable that someone will suffer a fate that they do not deserve. And God is utterly loving and nothing, either in life or death, can separate people from that love.

It matters in life

A choice to follow Jesus changes people. Christians speak of a clear sense of being accompanied and directed through life by an unseen presence. Awareness of the Holy Spirit indwelling a person is a real, albeit unspectacular, enrichment to life. In the New Testament, Paul described nine evident signs of the Holy Spirit bearing fruit in someone's life. A Christian can expect to register an increase in love, joy, peace, patience, kindness, goodness, faithfulness, gentleness and self-control.

A Christian sense of having found the purpose of his or her life is most clearly felt in activities that improve the circumstances of the world to increase in it the values of the Kingdom of God:

• **Pursuing justice.** The urgency with which Christians give money, campaign and pray on behalf of the world's poorest communities is more than kind-hearted charity. It is central to their faith that God desires a world in which justice is done. Working for human rights, seeking the end of oppression, and creating the circumstances in which people can rise from poverty are not desirable additions to the good news of Jesus; rather they are the good news.

• **Building peace.** The word peace is used in the Bible in a very broad sense that takes in the wellbeing and health of people, as well as the absence of violence. For a Christian this has an impact on the way they pray for the end of conflict between nations and religions. But it also impacts on their own behaviour as they promote harmony in their communities, families and anywhere that they can make a practical difference. It is not uncommon to hear Christians talk of their own inner peace, despite the difficulties that life throws at them.

• **Work and community.** In a society for which the loneliness of individuals and families is increasingly significant, one of the blessings of the Holy Spirit is that it draws people into community. When a local church is functioning effectively, people find in it friendship, encouragement, help in time of need, and opportunities to use their skills in the service of others. (It must be added, unfortunately, that in churches which are not functioning effectively it is possible to find only boredom and duty.) The shared sense of purpose that can be found in a church community has an impact that changes the way people regard their activity throughout the whole course of a week. Awareness that neighbours, friends and work colleagues are people loved by God can mean seeing them with kinder eyes. Work, leisure and routine tasks can become contexts for increasing the amount of joy in a world alive with awareness of God. It is as if Jesus Christ himself is being served.

want to know more?

• *Mere Christianity*, CS Lewis, HarperCollins, 2001
• *Simply Christian*, Tom Wright, SPCK, 2006
• www.christianity. org.uk
• www.life4seekers. co.uk

4 What Christians do

At the heart of Christian worship is obedience to Jesus' entreaty that he should be remembered by drinking wine and eating bread. Almost all Christians gather regularly to do so in the context of prayer, Bible study and mutual support. But although Christians seek inspiration in meeting together on a Sunday, it is in the community from day to day that their faith should mark them out. This chapter explains what Christians do in order to draw close to God and to act as servants to his world.

Christianity as a way of life

There is no system of obligations by which Christians live. The Christian faith is based on a relationship of love between people and God. To be a Christian is to live your life in the context of the sum total of all things. This is freedom, because there are no decrees that burden God's followers with fear of breaking them. However, gratitude for all that God has done leads to a desire to live in a godly way, and from that springs faith, service and prayer.

must know

One of the passages from the Bible that inspire Christians to a life of faith:

• Jesus said: 'Come to me, all you who are weary and burdened, and I will give you rest. Take my yoke upon you and learn from me, for I am gentle and humble in heart, and you will find rest for your souls.' (Matthew 11:28-29)

Faith

Christianity is distinct from some other religions in that there are no particular rituals, clothes or practices which mark out its adherents. This means that it is possible for many people to identify themselves as Christian without it appearing to make any day-to-day impact on their lives. Their relationship with the faith is based on the fact that they live in a society whose justice, welfare, seasons and culture have been shaped over many centuries by the principles that Jesus taught. The benefits of being nominally Christian are huge, because they have created a society in which, for the most part, vulnerable people do not rot unaided, or face execution without trial when they are a political inconvenience. And a Christian heritage accounts for much of what makes life joyful – public holidays such as Christmas, beauty in architecture and music, and contexts in which to welcome birth and face death.

However, those who allow Christianity to shape their lives in an active way explain that life is improved immeasurably by going through it in partnership with God. This requires faith, for God's existence is not open to proof or disproof. But their faith is not without evidence, because it expresses itself in a relationship with Jesus, their inspiration as a historical human and their hope as a living God. And that relationship provides the security, self-worth and purpose that create what Jesus called 'a life in all its fullness'.

A life of Christian faith allows people to experience the exhilaration, tragedy and humdrum of human experience in the context of an eternal existence. It provides for them to face bereavement or their own mortality in the assurance that they are in the company of a God who knows the way out of a tomb. It gives them someone to whom to say thank you for experiences for which an atheistic view of life seems inadequate, such as the creation of life, sacrificial love or gratuitous beauty. It provides a way of moving on from regret or wrongdoing through the forgiveness of God, freely offered to repentant people. And in times of anguish it gives reassurance that the God who has a good and just plan for the created order is going through the experience alongside them. Christians who choose a life of faith claim that their lives have both purpose and destiny, often describing their experience in terms of an inner peace and an absolute assurance of being loved.

Service

In the footsteps of Jesus, Christian lifestyle at its best is characterized by a desire to serve in a selfless way. In the teaching of Jesus, two metaphors stand out. He called his followers to be like salt and like light.

In comparing his followers to salt, which was at the time mainly used as a food preservative, Jesus sees them fully absorbed in their society, invisibly influencing it for good. It is in response to this challenge that Christians

must know

Another encouraging passage from the New Testament:
• Paul wrote: 'I know what it is to be in need, and I know what it is to have plenty. I have learned the secret of being content in any and every situation, whether well fed or hungry, whether living in plenty or in want. I can do everything through him who gives me strength.' (Philippians 4:12–13)

Some of the passages from the Bible that challenge Christians to service:

• Jesus said: 'You are the salt of the earth. But if the salt loses its saltiness, how can it be made salty again? It is no longer good for anything, except to be thrown out and trampled under foot. You are the light of the world. A city on a hill cannot be hidden. Neither do people light a lamp and put it under a bowl. Instead they put it on its stand, and it gives light to everyone in the house. In the same way, let your light shine before others, that they may see your good deeds and praise your Father in heaven.' (Matthew 5:13–16)

• Paul wrote: 'Love must be sincere. Hate what is evil; cling to what is good. Be devoted to one another in brotherly love. Honour one another above yourselves. Never be lacking in zeal, but keep your spiritual fervour, serving the Lord. Be joyful in hope, patient in affliction, faithful in prayer. Share with God's people who are in need. Practise hospitality.' (Romans 12:9–13)

involve themselves in charitable work and commit themselves to enriching the lives of vulnerable or lonely people. In contrast, when he called his followers 'the light of the world', Jesus had in mind the lights of a town guiding travellers safely on treacherous roads. This aspect of Christian lifestyle is associated with a more public advocacy of ethical standards and becomes explicit when Christians campaign on behalf of the poor or oppressed.

Christianity is essentially a community religion. From its earliest days, the church has been the word used to describe not a building nor an act of worship, but the local people following Jesus in a particular place. Almost all its benefits rise from being part of a group where giving, receiving, supporting and sharing come naturally. One of the New Testament writers described the church as a place where Christians would 'consider how we may spur one another on toward love and good deeds', and to facilitate this urged his readers: 'Let us not give up meeting together, as some are in the habit of doing, but let us encourage one another.' In this respect, belonging to a church is something that enriches daily life, not just the hour for public worship on a Sunday.

There is a tension between looking inward to help each other (maintenance) and looking outward in service to those in spiritual or practical need (mission). The former creates loving communities, but the latter is observed as something that warms people toward exploring their own relationship with God. Christians whose faith is active feel galvanized to both in response to the love of God. It is God's work done by human hands.

Prayer

Through the Holy Spirit, Christians recognize their lives and their world to be infused with God, enabling them to be in constant communication with him. A life of worship is one in which the true worth of God is made explicit in action, reflection and, above all, prayer.

In prayer, Christians become consciously aware that they are in the presence of God. In aligning themselves with the source and destiny of all things, they allow their innermost desires, fears and joys to be communicated to God, and they also make themselves open to God guiding and shaping them. In this respect, prayer is not simply a series of requests to the Creator to change the course of history to suit someone's personal needs; rather it is an active response to the unfolding will of God being worked out in the world. It can be expressed in words, in silent thought or in contemplative reading or listening. Although Christians actively seek God's answers to their prayers, they recognize this as often in a change to their own actions and perceptions as in a miraculous intervention.

This conversation with God is expressed as:

- **Praise**, which puts a human in their humble place compared with the God of utter love, justice and holiness.
- **Thanksgiving**, which recognizes that all that enriches life can be traced to the Creator.
- **Petition**, ranging in scope from the personal to the global.
- **Confession**, asking forgiveness for the damage they have done through their wrongdoing.
- **Seeking guidance**, direction, or understanding of the mysteries at the heart of existence.

must know

Jesus suggested a pattern for prayer to his followers which is recorded in the Bible. Its range of praise, petition, confession and submission to God's way have formed the basis of Christian prayer for many centuries. But 'The Lord's Prayer' is also recited corporately on many occasions when worshippers are together:

- 'Our Father in heaven, hallowed be your name.
Your kingdom come;
your will be done on earth as in heaven.
Give us today our daily bread.
Forgive us our sins as we forgive those who sin against us.
Lead us not into temptation, but deliver us from evil.
For the kingdom, the power, and the glory are yours, now and for ever. Amen.'

Christian worship

There is no such thing as a typical Christian service of worship. It can be sombre or jubilant, ornate or simple, sung or silent, following a written order or unpredictable. Worship develops to match the culture of those who seek to honour God through it. But there are some common features that Christians recognize no matter where in the world they join a church at prayer.

must know

A denomination is a strand of Christian tradition that brings together congregations into one organization that agrees certain core beliefs and practices. For instance, Roman Catholics form one denomination, Methodists another, and there are scores more. They are all Christian, and most seek to understand each other and co-operate, but differences of opinion have caused them to split from each other in past centuries.

Bread and wine

A fellowship meal as the context for remembering Jesus has been a central feature of the Christian church ever since his resurrection. In obedience to Jesus' plea on the night before he died that his followers should remember him by eating bread and drinking wine, Christians have done so throughout history.

In the early Christian years a full meal was shared on a Sunday, the day kept special because it was the day on which Jesus' tomb was discovered empty. However, the meal proved divisive. The New Testament includes a letter from Paul to the church at Corinth which criticizes gluttonous behaviour and the separation of rich and poor participants. Regulations were introduced in order to create a dignified and prayerful setting, specifying who could preside and in what circumstances people could take part. Prayers were devised to give a focus to the act of worship. Over time, the prayers became more significant and the meal less so, resulting in a service in which a token amount of bread and wine are consumed after prayers that allow worshippers to prepare themselves through praise and confession.

In different settings the service is known as Holy Communion, Mass (the term used in Roman Catholic and Orthodox churches), Eucharist (meaning thanksgiving), the Breaking of Bread or the Lord's Supper. But for all its variations of style, theology and type of bread or wine, communion remains the Christian's most powerful symbol of receiving the love of God, as hands are held out empty and food is placed in them.

Water

The water of baptism, which welcomes new followers of Jesus into the church, has two associations. Firstly it is a sign of having sin washed away – a clean start with the endlessly forgiving God, represented by pouring water over a person's head. Secondly it is a symbol of death, drowning the old life and rising to a new life with God – most clearly signified when the person being baptized is completely immersed in the water.

The New Testament records many baptisms. Some were of adults and some of entire families (presumably including children). Some were outdoors in rivers (in which the new Christian was immersed) and some indoors using water from storage jars (presumably involving water being poured, called affusion). The first Christian converts were baptized immediately they declared themselves to be followers of Jesus, but soon a period of preparation and learning over several months became common, with many baptisms taking place at the same time on Easter Sunday.

The diversity of experience in the New Testament is reflected in the practices of churches today. Most churches baptize infants who are born into families in which Jesus is honoured, because they will be brought up as Christians. In these circumstances it is the love of God that is being stressed, given even to those who cannot yet understand its significance. Parents and godparents (friends who commit themselves to bringing up the child to have faith in Jesus) make vows to follow Jesus on behalf of the infant, praying that as an adult the baptized person will make them for him- or herself. Historically, baptism of a baby has also been known as christening. Usually it involves the pouring of water from a large piece of furniture incorporating a basin, called a font. Eastern Orthodox churches, though, baptize babies by immersion.

In Pentecostal and Baptist churches, among others, parents of newborn children have a service of dedication, but baptism is reserved for adults who are old enough to have made their own informed and lasting decision to follow Jesus (believers' baptism). Under these circumstances it is the significance of baptism as an act of personal witness that is being stressed. Purpose-built churches where adult baptism takes place have a small pool, called a baptistery, for this purpose. In the developing world, a river or the sea is often used.

For the most part, churches address the confusion of this diversity by respecting each others' practices.

Sacraments

A sacrament is a tangible object or action that allows people to acknowledge and appreciate something that is real, but invisible – God drawing close to a human to change and enliven him or her. The water of baptism and the bread and wine of communion are familiar sacraments. Roman Catholic and Orthodox Christians recognise five other actions (which are familiar to all Christians) as having a special sacramental significance:

• **Marriage** – more than an exchange of vows; a vocation that requires God's grace.

• **Confirmation** – a service that completes in adulthood the commitment to the Christian faith that began in infancy with baptism.

• **Ordination** – setting apart as priests some who are particularly called to lead, teach and administer sacraments to the people of God.

• **Absolution** – an assurance of forgiveness for someone who has confessed a sin and needs to be rid of the burden of guilt.

• **Anointing** – the use of oil, placed on a sick person, as a visible token of prayer for healing (called last rites or extreme unction when a person is near death as they pass into wholeness in God's presence).

must know

Neither baptism nor communion feature in the worship of Quakers (the Society of Friends) or the Salvation Army. Quakers, who seek to be entirely inclusive, try to regard every meal as having the qualities of a sacrament. And the Salvation Army, which has always emphasized the need for God's grace over the need for rituals, has its own moments of deep significance, some involving their distinctive flag.

A world of worship

Christianity is a singing faith. The last time Jesus and his followers ate together, they sang a hymn, and since then public worship has usually involved God's people singing his praises together. Services have very different styles in all the countries of the world, reflecting the culture of the worshippers, but Christians recognize some common strands wherever they go – music extolling God, readings from the Bible, prayer for local and international needs, statements of faith, confession of sins. A sermon (of varying length and quality) interpreting the Bible is a frequent feature. Not every service includes communion – its frequency is not regarded as an indication of its importance.

Another familiar element of Christian worship is silence, which has a compelling power when people experience it together. It is used to contemplate the ways of God or to seek his direction through life, sometimes guided with thought-provoking readings. The worship of Quakers can be almost entirely silent, and there is also a tradition of meditation in places historically associated with monasteries.

A form of worship that is familiar in some places, but regarded with suspicion in others, is charismatic worship. As well as the other features of prayer, praise and learning, there is a direct experience of the Holy Spirit. A service of this kind includes time for people to say or sing prayers using words in languages unknown to the speaker. 'Speaking in tongues,' as it is known, is exuberant and mesmeric, and believed to be a gift granted by God. Sometimes all participate at once, and on other occasions an individual will speak unfamiliar words, with another person translating them. Other features of charismatic worship include prayer for healing, messages of encouragement or challenge that seem to be delivered directly from God, and times when worshippers sit or lie on the floor oblivious to anything except the uplifting love of Jesus. This warm and informal worship is a feature of Pentecostal denominations, but almost every denomination includes some congregations that feel themselves enriched by it.

As well as gathering in as large a number as possible for services of public worship, Christians also have a tradition of gathering in smaller groups to study the Bible together, tell the story of what God is doing in their lives, pray for each other, and organize charitable work to benefit vulnerable people locally or worldwide. It is in these groups that the hospitality, encouragement and practical help that improve people's lives in real terms takes place.

And the church is also the context in which Christians, whether they have a nominal faith or a vital and transforming belief, mark rites of passage such as weddings and funerals. Moments of national significance, such as remembrance of the sacrifices made in times of war or independence from colonial control, regularly take place in a Christian setting. Seeking the blessing of God, whether on vows, joyfulness or partings, comes naturally to vast numbers of people in countries with a history shaped by Christian beliefs.

must know

A prayer originally from the New Testament that is said by Christians of many persuasions in almost all the countries of the world:
• 'May the grace of the Lord Jesus Christ,
and the love of God,
and the fellowship of the Holy Spirit
be with us evermore.
Amen.'

Highlights of the Christian year

Christian worship recognizes that life in God's world has a rhythm, in which joy is followed by sorrow, anxiety is followed by celebration, and sometimes the emotions are confused together. Over the course of a year a calendar of special events remembers particular events in the life of Jesus, sometimes with quiet sadness and sometimes with joyful exuberance.

must know

The commercial demands of Christmas have changed the way it is celebrated. Originally, Advent was a time of abstinence, allowing Christmas to arrive with a rediscovery of the joys of feasting. This period of excess would last for 'the twelve days of Christmas' until Epiphany came as a climax involving the exchange of gifts. However, Advent is now more realistically associated with an accelerating programme of festivity, culminating on Christmas Day, with the days following Christmas something of an anticlimax, until 'twelfth night' (on Epiphany) sees decorations removed. Some Christians, dismayed by the meaninglessness of a secular Christmas, are seeking to revive the spirit of Advent as a time of prayer and attention to global injustice.

Advent

Meaning 'coming', Advent is a period of nearly four weeks leading up to Christmas. It is a period of spiritual preparation for Christmas, marking Jesus' original coming to this planet. However, it also focuses Christians' attention on the fact that Jesus is expected to return in a different and triumphant manner at his 'second coming', to establish ultimate justice. The tradition of counting down the days to Christmas on a colourful calendar is still widely practised, although few register its religious significance.

Christmas

Christmas Day, on 25 December, is celebrated as the anniversary of Jesus' birth. The actual date is not known, but Christians adopted the date of an older mid-winter festival. Orthodox Christians, following a different calendar, celebrate Christmas on 7 January. Christians make a point of taking communion on Christmas Day, often making it the first thing they do as the clock strikes midnight. Carols telling the story of Jesus' birth and associated Christmas legends feature in secular as well as religious culture.

Epiphany, meaning 'appearance', is marked on 6 January. It recalls the visit of magi (wise men) to Jesus, bearing gifts of gold, frankincense and myrrh. This was the first encounter between Jesus and people who were not Jewish (Gentiles) and is significant as the first sign that the work God was doing through Jesus was for the benefit of all humankind. Orthodox Christians use this day to focus on the baptism of Jesus, in which he identified himself completely with men and women in all their need. They mark the day by praying for God's blessing on local water sources, and it has greater significance than in UK churches, where it sometimes passes unnoticed.

Lent

For just over six weeks before Easter (40 days being the time that Jesus spent in the desert dwelling on the future shape of his ministry) Christians prepare by taking their spirituality particularly seriously. This involves prayer, confession of failings and a resolve to live in a more godly way. Historically this was marked by fasting. Still today it can involve sacrificing foods or activities that might be regarded as luxuries, as a spiritual discipline that puts prayer into sharper focus.

must know

There are several significant days during Lent:
- Shrove Tuesday is the day before Lent begins. Traditionally luxury foods, forsaken during Lent, were eaten on this day, a custom which is still marked by eating pancakes. 'Shrove' comes from an ancient word for seeking forgiveness. In much of the world the day is known as Mardi Gras (Fat Tuesday) and is a carnival day.
- Ash Wednesday is the first day of Lent. Many Christians attend church on this day, particularly to repent of wrongdoing. The priest places ash on the worshipper's forehead in the shape of a cross as a mark of being penitent.
- Mothering Sunday, the fourth Sunday in Lent, was in the sixteenth century a celebration to appreciate the motherly nature of the church, but has become a day for honouring all mothers.

Holy Week

The seven days before Easter are set aside to reflect on the death of Jesus. The week begins with Palm Sunday, during which Jesus' entry into Jerusalem, cheered by crowds as he rode a donkey, is remembered. Four days later, Maundy Thursday is marked in memory of the night before Jesus died, during which he instructed his followers to remember him by eating bread and drinking wine. The word Maundy derives from the Latin word for commandment, because it was during that evening that Jesus commanded his followers to love one another in the way he had loved them.

Good Friday, the most solemn day of the Christian year, is the Friday of Holy Week. Good Friday (or Holy Friday in predominantly Roman Catholic countries) is used to reflect on the appalling death of Jesus. In churches from which colour and splendour have temporarily been stripped, subdued and meditative services take place. Most countries with a Christian tradition observe Good Friday as a public holiday, although it is increasingly difficult to distinguish the day's activities from any other, so open-air services and processions are becoming common to allow churches to communicate the day's importance to their communities.

Easter Sunday

Christians celebrate the resurrection of Jesus from the dead during the most important and joyful festival of the year. Exultant music is performed, candles and fires are lit, and the centuries-old cry, 'Alleluia! Christ is risen!' is met with the response, 'He is risen indeed. Alleluia!'

must know

Holy Week has accumulated many traditions, with variations around the world.
• On Palm Sunday, crosses made from palm leaves are distributed to worshippers, recalling the palm leaves that a jubilant crowd waved to hail Jesus.
• Most Christians attend a service of communion at some point on Maundy Thursday.
• On Good Friday, spiced buns with the shape of a cross on the top (hot cross buns) are eaten in English-speaking countries.
• Easter Sunday has been seized on by retailers as an opportunity to sell chocolate Easter eggs and other luxury foods. For those who have observed Lent as a time of disciplined restraint, eating chocolate is a sign of rediscovering the joy of rich food in a world that God created and sustains. In various countries of the world, decorating eggs or hiding them for children to find are traditions in which the egg symbolizes the everyday miracle of the beginning of a new life.

At a very early date the Jews who were the first followers of Jesus changed their weekly day of worship from Saturday to Sunday in order to register the colossal significance of Easter, from which the hope and expectation of Christians that death is not the end derives. Easter Sunday has a variable date in late March or April because it is based (like Jewish calendars) on the occurrence of a full moon, and Orthodox churches celebrate it on a later date.

Forty days after Easter, on a Thursday, Christians mark Ascension Day and recall the final appearance of the risen Jesus to his followers. It is a day to acknowledge that Jesus is alive in heaven in the presence of God, a destiny that Christians share.

Pentecost

The pouring out of the Holy Spirit on the first followers of Jesus, beginning a new phase in the work of God in the world, is marked at Pentecost. It has an alternative name, Whitsun (meaning White Sunday). Christians use it to pray that, through the power that the Holy Spirit gives, they and the church will be effective channels for the good that God wants to do in the world. It takes place on a Sunday, 50 days after Easter. The name Pentecost has its roots in Jewish tradition, where it was originally a thanksgiving for a successful harvest. Christians too have a harvest festival on variable dates toward the end of summer, decorating churches with fruit, vegetables and loaves.

One week after Pentecost, Trinity Sunday sees teaching in churches that God the Creator, Jesus the Christ, and the Holy Spirit, although we speak of them as three Persons, are eternally one God.

want to know more?

- *What is the Point of Being a Christian?*, Timothy Radcliffe, Continuum, 2005
- *Detox Your Spiritual Life*, Peter Graystone, Canterbury Press, 2004
- *Nooma* DVD series, Rob Bell, Zondervan, 2005 onwards

5 The story of the Christian church

In the weeks after Jesus' resurrection, the number of his dedicated followers was thought to be 120. At the beginning of the twenty-first century, estimates put the number of worshipping Christians at just over 2 billion. Some parts of the story of the expansion of the church worldwide show it to have been an extraordinary force for good; other parts are frankly shameful. This chapter races through 2000 years of the history of the church.

The birth of the church

During its initial 300 years, the church experienced its first dramatic growth, its first persecutions and its first painful divisions because of theological disagreements (schisms). It had two distinct phases – the period when the eyewitnesses of Jesus' life led and organized the church and the subsequent period, when bishops oversaw it and kept the tradition alive.

Pentecost

With the suicide of Judas, the twelve whom Jesus had chosen as his closest associates (the apostles) became eleven. Jesus' final instruction to them had been to wait in Jerusalem and expect to be empowered, so they and about 100 others gathered together there regularly to pray. They made a decision to choose a new leader to bring the number of apostles back to twelve. Although Matthias, who was chosen, is not mentioned again in the New Testament, this event was significant because it created the possibility that someone who had not been one of Jesus' chosen twelve could become a leader of the group.

Pentecost, a Jewish harvest festival, brought an international crowd of Jews together as visitors to Jerusalem. For the followers of Jesus in the town that year it was an unexpectedly dramatic event. They became inflamed with an ecstatic fervour, creating such an uproar in their worship that a crowd gathered. Peter, taking the initiative as their spokesman, addressed the throng explaining that the cause was the Spirit of God inhabiting them as never before.

must know

The date of Jesus' birth has always been a matter of speculation because the evidence is contradictory. Most historians suggest that it was about 4 BC. In the sixth century a Romanian monk named Dionysius attempted to calculate the date, and on the basis of his conclusions BC (Before Christ) and AD (Anno Domini, 'the year of the Lord') have remained the turning points of calendars used in countries where Christianity is the major religion. But he probably got it wrong.

The Holy Spirit was referred to many times in the Hebrew Scriptures to describe God intervening in the affairs of the world. Peter identified the extraordinary event that had taken place as a new phase in God's unfolding plan. God had poured out the Holy Spirit on all people. Peter went on to preach about Jesus, announcing that he was the Messiah and had been raised from the dead. Declaring that everyone present was implicated in the tragedy of Jesus' death, he explained that they could all be forgiven if they repented and were baptized.

About 3000 responded, radically increasing the size of the first church. Over the coming weeks more joined them, attracted by the joy of their fellowship – praying and eating together, sharing possessions in response to people's needs, and listening to the apostles tell them about Jesus.

Opposition

The idyllic life of the first church was short lived because of problems both inside and outside the group. Its rapid growth unsettled the religious leaders, who feared that a heretical sect within Judaism would grow – the very thing they had tried to stop by killing Jesus. They issued threats and the apostles had spells in prison.

The twelve apostles found that their workload was multiplying as the numbers grew, with the result that some within the group grumbled that they were getting a raw deal when the apostles shared out food. Seven more people were appointed to oversee the pastoral care of the believers. One of these, Stephen, became involved in a battle of words with members of the Sanhedrin (the Jewish council),

must know

Antioch, 300 miles north of Jerusalem, became a substantial centre for the worship of Jesus following the scattering of his persecuted followers. It was here that they first became known as Christians (perhaps sarcastically at first, but adopted with pride).

which escalated when the leaders interpreted his vision of Jesus and God standing shoulder to shoulder as blasphemy. With fury rising, Stephen was dragged outside the city and stones were thrown at him until he was dead.

This unleashed an onslaught of persecution against the followers of 'the Way'. The apostles stayed in Jerusalem, but many others fled in fear for their lives, north, south and across the sea. However, this dispersion served only to take the story of what Jesus had said and done further afield. Wherever they went, the believers made contact with fellow Jews, announcing that the Messiah had come, had died and was risen. Small gatherings of Jews began to worship Jesus in many towns, even as far afield as Rome, the capital of the world's superpower.

The Jewish leaders responded by appointing one of their finest intellectuals, a Roman citizen from Tarsus (present-day Turkey), to stop the spread of the sect. His name was Saul. With a fury, he set about detaining anyone who worshipped Jesus. However, while on his way from Jerusalem to Damascus with arrest warrants in his hand, he had a life-changing vision during which he became convinced that he had encountered the risen Jesus. Frightened and temporarily blinded, he was led to Damascus, where he astonished the followers of Jesus by publicly declaring that he believed Jesus to be the Son of God. Understandably, this made him a target of many Jews' rage, and he was spirited away first to Jerusalem and then home to Tarsus.

Saul started a long period of scriptural study in Tarsus and became convinced that Jesus was the one to whom the Old Testament pointed. At some point he changed his name from Saul to Paul (the nearest Roman equivalent), and this period prepared him for his world-changing role as a pioneering missionary. With the collapse of Paul's vendetta against the followers of Jesus, they had a period of stability, and their numbers continued to grow.

Jews and Gentiles

The spread of the good news about Jesus presented the Christians with an unexpected problem. They had anticipated that only Jews would find the way of Jesus compelling. However the evidence was that, when introduced to the news that Jesus was risen, Gentiles responded in the same ecstatic way that the apostles had on the day of Pentecost. The Holy Spirit of God was clearly indwelling men and women regardless of their religion. In particular Peter became convinced that Gentiles should be incorporated into the church.

The same issue emerged in Antioch, and Paul was identified as the person with the wisdom to help both Jews and Gentiles work out the implications of the new circumstances. He came from Tarsus to Antioch. After a year he and fellow travellers set off to towns in present-day Turkey and Cyprus, preaching to both Gentiles and Jews. Everywhere they left new converts in their trail.

They arrived back to another controversy. It was unclear whether Gentiles who became Christians should also be required to become Jews and embrace Jewish dietary laws and circumcision. Paul believed they should not, as did Peter, but there were heated arguments with others. The apostles called the leaders of the churches in various towns together in Jerusalem to debate this in about AD 50.

The argument that prevailed was that being a Christian was a matter of being put right with God because of what Jesus had done. This was God's gracious gift, and did not require obedience to any set of laws in order to earn it. No additional obstacle should confront Gentiles when they responded in faith to Jesus.

This decision was momentous because it changed Christianity from a sect within Judaism (which would have struggled to endure) into a religion that could cross all cultural and national boundaries.

During the second century a statement of belief was used to help converts to Christianity understand the essentials of their faith. It was known as the Apostles' Creed and is still used today:

• 'I believe in God, the Father almighty, creator of heaven and earth.

'I believe in Jesus Christ, his only Son, our Lord, who was conceived by the Holy Spirit, born of the Virgin Mary, suffered under Pontius Pilate, was crucified, died, and was buried. He descended to the dead. On the third day he rose again. He ascended into heaven, he is seated at the right hand of the Father, and he will come to judge the living and the dead.

'I believe in the Holy Spirit, the holy catholic church, the communion of saints, the forgiveness of sins, the resurrection of the body and the life everlasting.'

Persecution and heresy

Driven with a fervour to make Jesus Christ known, Paul spent the next fifteen years travelling through towns north of the Mediterranean. The last mention of him in the New Testament has him in Rome, under house arrest and longing for his day in court before the emperor, boldly preaching and writing about Jesus at the hub of the known world.

His travels took place in the context of a famine in and around Jerusalem, to which Christians in other places responded with financial help. There was sometimes persecution, but this was sporadic because there was as yet no policy in the Roman Empire toward an apparently insignificant movement. It was as Christianity came to be dominated by Gentiles that major opposition began. In Rome, Jews were excused from offering incense as an act of worship to the emperor, but a mainly Gentile religion could not claim that the exemption covered them. When a fire destroyed much of the city, the emperor Nero put the blame on the new Christian sect. Because they ate bread and drank wine, declaring it to be Jesus' body and blood, they were accused of cannibalism. The purge that followed was brief but bloody and it is assumed that among the victims in AD 65 were Paul and Peter.

Attacks from outside served only to strengthen the Christians. Attacks from within were more damaging. Without an agreed set of doctrines, Christians in far-flung towns found themselves under the influence of whoever's teaching was most compelling. If a preacher encouraged the worship of angels (as someone did in Colossae – a typical 'gnostic' belief) there was no reason to suspect that this was an aberrant belief until Paul wrote a letter to the church making it clear. Paul insisted that the Christian gospel was not a secret way known only to a few, but a gift of God available to all. He urged that anyone burdening followers of Jesus with additional requirements should be ignored or expelled.

The need for confidence in orthodox expressions of the faith was growing, and it was in response to this that the documents that make up the New Testament Scriptures were written, creeds that expressed the basic beliefs were agreed, and a pattern of authorized ministry was developed during the second century. By establishing the orders of bishop, priest (sometimes known as a presbyter) and deacon, the church protected itself from eccentric variations of the teaching that the apostles passed on from Jesus taking hold.

With consolidation came a problem for those who had principled beliefs that were not accepted by those overseeing orthodoxy. With increasing numbers came the temptation to form breakaway groups.

For example, one of the debates in this period was about whether increasing organization was smothering the spontaneity that the Holy Spirit had unlocked in the first believers. Toward the end of the second century Montanus, in present-day Turkey, practised a form of Christianity that featured ecstatic language ('speaking in tongues') and emotional prophecy through which it was claimed that God was communicating directly with people. This form of worship contrasted with the sobriety of the official church. When a highly respected theologian, Tertullian, joined the Montanists its popularity as a sect within Christianity grew, and the mainstream church denounced it. The name persisted for four centuries, but the questions the group raised never went away. Still today the Christian church struggles to hold together spontaneity and order.

must know

The text of a letter to a man called Diognetus has survived from about 200, revealing much about how Christians in North Africa were regarded:

• 'Christians are no different from the rest of mankind. They do not live in cities of their own or have a different language or way of life ... but the way they live is marvellous and confounds all expectations ... They have children, but they don't kill the unwanted ones. They eat with all their neighbours, but they don't sleep with all their neighbours ... They love all people, even though they are persecuted by all people ... They are poor, but they enrich other people's lives ... Their existence is on earth, but they are citizens of heaven.'

Faith and empire

The appropriate relationship between Christians and the society in which they lived also divided Christians. Alongside other despised minorities, thousands of Christians perished in arenas in spectator sports. The memory and the actual remains of martyrs were venerated. Some saw the State as wicked and greeted martyrdom as an honour. Others were keen to engage with the culture – Justin Martyr, for instance, responded to persecution by writing to the emperor arguing that Christians were misunderstood and had a high morality that should be allowed to flourish. Christian intellectuals emerged, such as Origen, and took on pagan philosophers on their own terms.

In this setting the lives of ordinary Christians continued to make a distinctive impact. The church bridged gulfs of class and gender, with men and women, the slaves and the wealthy, worshipping side by side. A commitment to alleviate poverty featured in the shared life of the church, as did an opposition to militarism. From the very first, however, there was diffidence about sex among Christians. Committed to marriage as its appropriate setting, there was a suggestion that chastity was even more virtuous.

Persecution continued, with a particularly vicious attempt by Emperor Diocletian at the beginning of the fourth century to halt Christianity's growth. However, in 312 Constantine defeated his rival at the battle of Milvian Bridge and became emperor. He attributed his victory to the blessing of Jesus, whom his mother Helena worshipped and to whom he had prayed for help. There was a certain amount of convenience in his espousal of Christianity, because he recognized that it was a force that could unite the fragmenting Roman empire. However, his intention that the faith should thrive in peace was genuine, and as a result of his patronage Christianity was at first officially tolerated and, by the end of that century, became the official religion of the empire.

The rise of Christendom

With Christianity the State religion, the bishop of Rome found himself in a position of real power and privilege. The church had to adapt to being popular, which brought a different set of problems. For 1000 tumultuous years the church was, for good or ill, the most influential organization on the planet.

Determining doctrine

Emperor Constantine supported the Christian church financially. He also took an active role in supporting its leadership on occasions when unity was threatened. One of the pressing issues was how to deal with Christians who had forsaken their faith during the years of persecution. It was a particular issue in North Africa where one of the bishops was caught up in the controversy, leading local Christians to elect someone else instead. Constantine judged in favour of the bishop who had originally been chosen, but did not succeed in enforcing it, so the sect continued appointing its own bishops.

It brought into focus a question that still troubles the church today: when there is division over a matter of principle, does authority lie with a local congregation (who might break away) or with the broad majority (who might have to suppress the dissenting group)? Augustine, who was the bishop of Hippo in present-day Algeria eight decades later, urged that the whole church had authority over any one part. But even his outstanding leadership could not prevent the weakening of the church in North Africa, which dwindled as Islam advanced in the eighth century.

In 325, Constantine called together the leaders of the church at Nicaea (in present-day Turkey) for its first international council. Its objective was to define orthodox

Augustine came back
to the Christian faith
which his mother had
taught him after years
as a brilliant student
in which his weakness
for sex and drink got
the better of him.
Looking back on that
time, he wrote these
words about Jesus:
• 'How late I came to
love you, O beauty so
ancient and so fresh,
how late I came to
love you! You were
within me while I had
gone outside to seek
you ... You called, you
cried, you shattered
my deafness. You
sparkled, you blazed,
you drove away my
blindness. You shed
your fragrance, and
I drew in my breath,
and I pant for you.
I tasted and now I
hunger and thirst. You
touched me, and now
I burn with longing for
your peace.'

Christianity and thus prevent more schisms. In
particular, it sought to stamp out the views of a priest
called Arius, whose teaching that Jesus was inferior to
God the Father had gained such popularity that it was in
danger of splitting the church. Out of this, and
subsequent councils at Constantinople in 381 (formerly
Byzantium, now Istanbul) and Chalcedon in 451 (also in
Turkey) came decisions that have shaped the way
Christian theology has been explained ever since. An
Egyptian man called Athanasius played a key role in
establishing the foundations of Christian understanding
that have endured through the centuries.

One of the decisions concerned the nature of Jesus.
Different schools of thought associated with different
cities emphasized either the humanity or the divinity of
Jesus. The councils determined that Jesus was not a split
personality who was half man and half god, but one
person who uniquely had two natures.

Another discussion centred on the relationship
between God the Father, Jesus Christ, and the Holy Spirit
– all of whom were worshipped as God. The decision was
that the Christian faith did not have three gods. There is
one God, an inseparable Trinity, in which the Son and the
Spirit were 'one essence' with the Father.

The broad agreements of the councils, published as
the Nicene Creed, came at a cost. A large, powerful
church found it harder to be true to its founder than a
small, suffering one. Personal rivalries led to bruising
encounters. The simplicity with which the first followers
of Jesus responded to him could readily be obscured as
intellectual abstractions ballooned. And despite
everyone's best efforts, some could not be reconciled to
the orthodoxy that prevailed. In particular one group, the
Monophysites, broke away. Their successors still have

their own denominations, forming the Oriental Orthodox Church, in Ethiopia, Egypt and elsewhere today.

Monasteries and missionaries

For many decades Christians who recognized that popularity did not necessarily make for integrity had sought to escape the political arguments of the church. The self-denial that might, in a previous generation, have led to martyrdom was leading some Christians to seek an austere way of life. For Anthony of Egypt at the turn of the fourth century, it led to the lifestyle of a hermit in the desert. Others followed and set up communities that focused on prayer in a rigorously disciplined way – the Desert Fathers. One of them, Jerome, devoted himself to translating the Bible into Latin, making it far more accessible than before.

The concept of Christian community flourished, and monasteries began to multiply – places of contemplation, study and mysticism. Later in the century, Basil of Caesarea founded monasteries and convents in which service to the poorest in society was as prominent as spirituality. A movement that had begun in the east became influential in western Europe as well, under John Cassian (in present-day France) and Benedict (a century later in southern Italy), whose Benedictine Rule set a pattern of work balanced with prayer that became standard in monasteries.

In 410, with Rome under attack from the Visigoths, the empire disintegrated. Leo I, bishop of Rome, had an international significance that the emperor could no longer claim, so his power increased. However, bishops in places far-flung from Rome were not all convinced that the church in the place where Christianity was first legalized was necessarily pre-eminent. Many miles east of Europe, a thoroughly resilient Christian tradition, the Byzantine Church, had developed its own distinct culture with its leader (called a Patriarch) based in Constantinople. Further conflict was inevitable.

However, invaders also brought with them opportunities to evangelize new groups of people. Although Vikings, Moguls and Vandals rolled back the influence of the Roman Empire, a generation of missionaries realized that the Kingdom of God was not only bigger than the Empire, it was bigger than time itself.

This had a profound significance for the islands that now form the United Kingdom. There were Christians in the British Isles very soon after Jesus' resurrection, but invading Saxons in the fifth century drove them west and north, making England mostly pagan. Christianity put down deep roots in Ireland, especially aided by the energetic activity of Patrick. As a young man he was taken from north-west England to Ireland as a slave, but his faith grew in that setting. He escaped to France, studied, became a bishop, and returned to Ireland to bring the gospel to people who had enslaved him.

Ireland became one of two centres from which missionaries set out to convert England, Scotland and Wales. In the middle of the sixth century Columba sailed from Ireland to Iona, in the Hebrides, where he founded a monastery. From there the monks set out to convert the Scottish people to Christianity. In the seventh century monks from Iona, Aidan and later Cuthbert, crossed the country and made their base on the island of Lindisfarne, in north-east England. These Celtic missionaries had a profound impact on the country, introducing Jesus to people in a way that honoured, instead of overriding, the existing culture.

must know

Athanasius, a bishop in Egypt in the fourth century, wrote this of Jesus' incarnation:
• 'He became what we are that he might make us what he is.'

The other centre from which missionaries advanced was Canterbury. At the end of the sixth century, Gregory was an enlightened bishop of the church in Rome, seeking peace with those who threatened the city, building hospitals, and promoting understanding between diverging groups of churches. He sent a missionary named Augustine to England with instructions that his approach should not be to destroy pagan worship sites, but instead to transform them into places where Jesus was venerated. A scared and reluctant Augustine arrived in Kent. The local queen, Bertha, had come from France to marry Ethelbert and was a Christian. She invited Augustine and his monks to make their home in Canterbury. Her husband, the king, converted to Christianity and his subjects followed in their thousands.

Two strands of Christian practice were flourishing in the islands. They organized their monasteries in different ways, celebrated Easter on a different date, and had other differences that now seem abstruse but were passionately contested (such as how a monk should cut his hair). In 644 the most significant English Christian leader of the time, a woman named Hilda, was asked to host a synod (a decision-making council) at her monastery in Whitby. These matters were discussed and Roman Christianity, with its highly organized structure, prevailed. This decision tied church tradition to that of mainland Europe for many centuries.

must know

Celtic Christianity emphasized contemplation of the Trinity and encouraged godliness to permeate attitudes to the environment and to every workaday activity. Its influence never went away and interest in it revived intensely at the start of the twenty-first century.

Power and division

The power of the bishop of Rome (known from the end of the sixth century as the Pope, or Father) continued to grow. However, the Byzantine Orthodox churches in the east (based in Constantinople) were also growing in a

must know

The church at the end of the first millennium was a monolith caught in a destructive power struggle. But most people were remote from such concerns. Local churches and monasteries usually had a positive impact on their communities. For those who survived by tough manual labour in a world threatened by barely understood diseases, the church was a mainstay. Sunday worship and festivals broke the monotony. The church organized care for the poor, sick and dying, and provided a supportive community. There was prayer in times of anxiety and celebration in times of joy. Most ordinary people were believers, and although Jesus would have been bewildered by extremists dealing with their temptations by beating the sin out of themselves, he would have recognized the generosity and love of Christian people as his own values.

different way. Under the leadership of their Patriarch, missionaries were taking Christianity to present-day Russia and the Balkans. They translated the Bible into the vernacular and helped people to worship in their own language (unlike their Roman counterparts who used Latin for many centuries). One of the distinctive features of their tradition was condemning portraits of Jesus (icons) as idolatrous, and many beautiful works of art were destroyed.

However, in Rome the dream was growing of a magnificent culture, unified by the Christian faith, in which the religion and the government were one. When, in 800, Pope Leo III crowned Charlemagne with the title Holy Roman Emperor, he created Christendom. This new empire had a Pope with unprecedented control and a warrior-king who was willing to use violence to expand church and empire together. And the rightness of this state of affairs was 'proved' by a document called *The Donation of Constantine* (presumed to date from the fourth century) which indicated that the first Christian emperor intended it all to work out this way. (It was a fake, but it was 600 years before that was acknowledged.)

Charlemagne's coronation made plain the differences between the Latin-speaking Christians in the Roman tradition and the Greek-speaking Christians in the Byzantine tradition. As decades went by, tensions about the authority of the Pope and the destruction of icons mounted. However, when a traumatic split came (the Great Schism) it was triggered by disagreement over a single word in the Nicene Creed about the relationship of Jesus and the Holy Spirit. In 1054 the Patriarch and the Pope excommunicated each other and two denominations went their separate ways – a tragic fracture between the world's Orthodox and Roman Catholic Christians.

The Crusades

At the end of the eleventh century Pope Gregory VII saw himself as a reformer, seeking to protect the church from the interference of the emperor and the laxity of clergy. There was a rise in theology as an intellectual discipline, with Anselm, the Archbishop of Canterbury, seeking to underpin faith with reason. However, the preoccupation of Christian leaders was the rise of Islam and, specifically, the fact that Turks had occupied Jerusalem – a city revered by Muslims because of its association with Muhammad.

Gregory's successor Pope Urban II urged and financed a military Crusade to retake the lands in which Jesus had lived. There was fervent enthusiasm in response to his call to arms. This was partly prompted by his promise of benefits to Crusader families and that fatally wounded warriors would go straight to heaven. In 1099 the first crusade succeeded in conquering Jerusalem.

However, under Saladin, Islam grew in strength as a religious and cultural force and 90 years later the Holy Land was ruled by Muslims again. The Crusades continued into the fifteenth century. They generated partial victories, tragic failures, appalling bloodshed and a shameful legacy that continues to blight the attempts of races and religions to live side by side in the present-day Middle East.

Power and change

There is little evidence of the humble style of leadership that Jesus advocated in the struggles of the medieval Popes for the right to impose taxes.

A series of French Popes in the fourteenth century found Avignon a safer and more luxurious place than Rome from which to rule. Factions that agitated for and against the Pope led to the excommunication of whole cities, and forced a move back to Rome. But there were divisions among the cardinals (senior bishops), some of whom grew so discontent that they elected a rival Pope. Armed battles followed, movements to make the power of the papacy subservient to councils of Christian leaders failed, and at one point three contenders claimed to be Pope at the same time.

This dismal state was relieved by the life-enhancing influence of the monasteries. They were centres of education, craftsmanship and care for the marginalized. From an isolated part of France, Cistercian monks planted hundreds of communities that rediscovered the rule that Benedict had established – austerity, hard work and charity. In the twelfth century Bernard, abbot of Clairvaux, was their inspirational leader. The Carthusian order of monks emphasized silence in their life of prayer and preached that 'the cross is steady while the world is turning'.

Many monasteries, through excellent management, became prosperous. In contrast, Francis of Assisi renounced wealth and founded a community in present-day Italy. Charming, kind and humble, he readily gathered followers to share his commitment to live like and serve the poor. His order were friars who, unlike monks, were free to move out of their monasteries and engage with the world, rather than retreat from it. The Franciscan order, and the complementary female order founded by in Assisi by Clare, still thrive. So does the Dominican order, founded by Dominic in the thirteenth century to add education to the priorities of Francis' mission. The finest of the Dominican thinkers was Thomas Aquinas, a friar who set his brilliant intellect to the task of proving that God exists.

But alongside the rigour of a scholarly approach to Christianity, there was a rise in a more personal and mystical response to Jesus. Mystics of the late fourteenth century included Julian, a woman who, alone in a sealed room built on the side of a church in Norwich, wrote inspirational accounts of what God had revealed to her of his good and loving plan for humankind. Her deep spirituality was typical of a search by many people for a personal engagement with God that bore little relation to the power and privilege that the institution of the church seemed to represent.

Mediaeval Christian leaders in their own words

- Francis: 'In the name of holy love, which is God, I implore all my brothers to lay aside every obstacle, every care, every trouble, and to serve, love, adore and honour the Lord with all their might, with a pure heart and a whole mind which he seeks above all.'
- Clare: 'O holy poverty, to those who possess and desire you, God promises the kingdom of heaven, and offers eternal glory and blessed life.'
- Julian: 'It is true that sin is the cause of all this pain, but all shall be well, and all shall be well, and all manner of things shall be well.'

Reformation and Enlightenment

At the beginning of the sixteenth century, Europeans were realizing that the world was different from anything they had known. Voyages of discovery had uncovered peoples and nations previously unimagined. The way men and women thought was changing too. A revival of the values of classical civilizations that pre-dated Jesus impacted on education, art and politics. 'The Renaissance' was changing the culture of Europe and change in the Western church was bound to follow.

must know

• Catholic is shorthand used to mean the Roman Catholic denomination, but without the capital letter, catholic means universal (above all divisions), which should be the aspiration of all Christian churches.
• Justification means being freed from the guilt or penalty of sin, and restored to a right relationship with God both in life and death.

Radical change

The church needed to be renewed. Its senior leaders were political tacticians. Some of its local leaders were impoverished; others were poor models for Christian morality. And the monasteries were beginning to decline.

However, the seeds of reform had been sown many years before. At the end of the twelfth century the insistence of the Archbishop of Canterbury, Thomas Becket, that the church should be independent of the monarchy cost him his life. Three centuries later Jan Hus met the same fate in the present-day Czech Republic, having insisted that the Bible has a greater authority than any church leader. In southern France Peter Waldo had founded a Christian movement that rejected luxury, rituals and eventually the church altogether. In England in the fourteenth century, John Wycliffe and his followers (the Lollards) attacked corruption in the church, urged that Christians should be properly taught so that they understood their faith and encouraged reading of the Bible in English instead of Latin so that all (not just the educated) could comprehend. And all strands of Christian tradition had within them devout, contemplative people who sought to shape their lives by the example of Jesus, notably Thomas à Kempis whose fifteenth-century book *The Imitation of Christ* was, and remains, a bestseller.

So in many ways the world was ready for a young German priest who earnestly sought to be at peace with God, but found the route to forgiveness was obscured, not fostered, by the Catholic church. Martin Luther found in the Bible a life-changing reassurance that sins could be forgiven and men and women could be at one with God. This was God's gift, made possible by Jesus, and required nothing in response but faith that it was so. In contrast, Luther observed in the church an attempt to sell God's pardon to those who could afford it (a system called 'indulgences'). His fury with a church that was, he believed, misleading people into paying them money for something that God offers without cost finally drove him to radical action. Luther wrote a 95-point essay and sent it to the Pope. He was ordered never to discuss his views with anyone. In response he had thousands of copies distributed in 1517 and nailed one of them to the door of Wittenberg Cathedral. To the surprise of the church, a spiritually hungry population rose to support him.

At a council of the church in Worms, he was excommunicated. He was tried for heresy, but escaped before he could be sentenced and was spirited away to Wartburg. There he translated the Bible into German, wrote prodigiously, and saw his movement to reform the church from within grow.

> **must know**
> • Excommunicate means to expel someone from a church by refusing them the bread and wine of communion.
> • Relic means a bone of a saint or an object associated with Jesus (such as a supposed splinter from his cross) preserved in a church to be venerated in worship.

However, the church was resistant to change and a break was inevitable. Lutheran churches spread rapidly, particularly in Germany and Scandinavia. Their desire was to sweep away additions to the Christianity that is found in the New Testament, such as indulgences, relics and Purgatory. They sought to make the church a setting that put people in touch with God, instead of being the gatekeeper that controlled people's access to God. The consequence was a division of the Western churches into Roman Catholic and Protestant churches that has persisted for five centuries.

The Reformation in Europe

In other parts of Europe, reformation of the church was taking place at the same time – with liberation, argument, and sometimes violence. In Switzerland, Ulrich Zwingli's thinking was even more radical than Luther's. He too preached that faith in Jesus allowed people to be reconciled to God (justified) and that Jesus was spiritually present in the bread and wine of communion (not actually and miraculously present, as the Catholic church holds). His plain, whitewashed chapels were a contrast to opulent churches full of icons, and his influence endures today in Reformed churches. He lost his life in violence against Catholic troops near Zurich.

In France, John Calvin encountered Luther's teaching and took it to Geneva. There, in the middle of the sixteenth century, he established a training academy from which leaders spread Protestant theology throughout Europe. He taught that God has known from the far recesses of eternity who was predestined to come to faith, and who would reject

must know

• The Renaissance is the name given to the period of transition from the mediaeval world to the modern world between the fourteenth and seventeenth centuries. It was marked by a revival of learning, art and literature, and took its inspiration from the great classical civilizations of Jesus' time and before.

• Humanism was a movement in the sixteenth century that brought the new spirit of the Renaissance to bear on Christianity, improving understanding of the Bible and criticizing the practices of the church by exploring the Christian heritage. The leading theologian associated with humanism was the Dutchman Desiderius Erasmus. (Present-day humanism has changed its meaning, and is now often associated with atheism.)

him. His quiet gift was to systematize the beliefs of the reformers and his legacy is a strict (some would say narrow) account of what it means for a Christian to find salvation that is held in high regard by Protestant churches with a conservative outlook today.

In other parts of Europe a more extreme 'radical Reformation' bypassed intellectual consideration of theology and depended on the Holy Spirit to communicate directly. Advocating baptism of adults, rather than infants who were too young to understand, they sought to recreate the communal lifestyle of the first church in Jerusalem, completely independent from the State. However, they were opposed by both Catholics and Protestants, and violence again ensued. Their influence can still be seen today in Anabaptist Christian groups, such as the Amish and the Brethren.

The Reformation in England, Scotland and Ireland

In every European country, the Reformation of the church was turbulent, mixing spiritual reawakening with political manoeuvring. However, in England this was most obvious (and most bloody) of all. Henry VIII was so adamantly anti-Luther that the grateful Pope declared him to be 'Defender of the Faith'. So it was a surprise to King Henry when Pope Clement VII refused to dissolve his marriage so that he could take a younger wife who was more likely to bear him a male heir. In 1534 Henry pronounced himself head of the Church of England. The Pope excommunicated him and Henry set about establishing a new structure that made clear his

must know

Over 200 men and women were executed in England during the Reformation years, refusing to renounce what was important in their faith.

• The Protestant Thomas Cranmer, who wrote the *Book of Common Prayer*, which has shaped and beautified the way Christians have prayed ever since, died in Oxford during Queen Mary's reign.

• William Tyndale, a Protestant, perished in the cause of making the Bible available to people in English, so that its message would not be constrained by the interpretation put on it by clergy who could read Latin.

• Margaret Clitherow, a Catholic who had hidden priests on the run during Elizabeth I's reign, died in York rather than have her children forced to appear in court and testify.

must know

must know

Three of the most
important principles that
drove the thinking of the
Reformers were:

• God is continually
speaking to humankind in
the present through the
ancient words of the Bible,
which is the measure of
whether a religious belief
is true.

• There is a single, unique
way for human beings to
become acceptable to God,
and that is because God
has taken the initiative
through his undeserved
and gracious love. No
mountain of good deeds
can earn salvation; solely
faith in Jesus.

• All men and women are,
in a sense, priests – serving
God through whatever
secular way of life
occupies them.

supremacy in church affairs, funding it by
ransacking and then closing the country's
monasteries. His actions created a space in which a
religious movement that had been growing strength
for nearly two centuries could thrive. The Lollard
tradition associated with John Wycliffe in the
fourteenth century had regained momentum when
Bibles in English were smuggled into the country
from Germany. A protest movement against the
Pope and a number of unspiritual clergy continued
to grow (Protestants). Henry VIII's successor was his
young son, Edward VI. During his time, under the
guidance of Thomas Cranmer, the Archbishop of
Canterbury, the Protestant Reformation took hold.

Brutal years followed as Edward was succeeded
by Mary, a devout but intolerant Catholic. Her
half-sister became Elizabeth I and restored
Protestantism as the national religion. Many
Christian leaders, both Catholic and Protestant, paid
with their lives for their convictions.

In Scotland, a Catholic priest called John Knox
converted to Protestantism and survived two years
as a galley slave in France before studying with
Calvin and returning home in 1559 to father the
Church of Scotland. 'The Kirk' (as it was known) was
different in many ways from the Church of England,
notably that the monarch was not and is not
established as its Governor. In Ireland, the
Reformation was imposed on the nation by the
English, an act which linked Protestantism
inseparably with foreign rule. The tragic
consequences of this continued for over four
centuries as opposing sides in the conflicts over the
political governance of the island defined

themselves by their denomination, Catholic or Protestant.

The church that emerged in England from this turmoil was unique and broad. It had members with a strong Protestant theology, others who looked back to the early years of the church for their inspiration, and elements that retained Catholic structure – special clothes for clergy leading services (vestments), particular words and patterns for worship (liturgy), and bishops.

For dogmatic Protestants this represented compromise, and it is from their dissatisfaction that the Puritan movement emerged and a tradition of nonconformists (dissenters) rose. It was the inability of the Puritans to retain their integrity in the emerging religious mainstream that led some of them, the Pilgrim Fathers, to leave England in 1620 to seek religious freedom in North America.

A Counter-Reformation

While Henry VIII was destroying the monasteries of England, a process of reform within the Catholic church accelerated in response. A damning report in 1537 revealed abuses in the church and recommended sweeping changes. Born in Loyola, Spain, a former soldier named Ignatius began a personal mission of reform. He founded the Society of Jesus (Jesuits), who offered people a new intensity in their relationship with God. Their devotional path was practical, disciplined and rooted in reality, but empowered by a dynamic encounter with Scripture.

For some years there was promise of reconciliation between the Roman Catholic and Protestant churches as eminent theologians sought

must know

A prayer of Ignatius of Loyola:
• Teach us, good Lord, to serve thee as thou deservest;
To give, and not to count the cost;
To fight, and not to heed the wounds;
To toil, and not to seek for rest;
To labour, and not to ask for any reward save that of knowing that we do thy will.

agreement. However, in the middle of the sixteenth century the leaders of the Catholic church met at Trent (northern Italy) and the result of their discussions was a narrowing of attitudes. Latin, rather than vernacular languages, was reaffirmed as the language for worship and Bible study, and the importance of the centuries-old tradition of the church was reasserted alongside the Bible in matters of theology. A new ruthlessness emerged in countering dissent. Under Pope Paul IV the Inquisition, which for centuries had been the department of the Catholic church charged with rooting out heresy, became a feared and lethal force.

A hardened church ensured its survival. There was a new passion and confidence, and a deep concern for the poor, led by compassionate people such as Vincent de Paul. The depth of spirituality can still be seen in the mystical devotional writings of Teresa of Avila and John of the Cross. There was also a courageous expansion of missionary activity, with Jesuits introducing the gospel to Paraguay and Brazil and – less successfully – to Africa, and Francis Xavier leading missions to India and Japan. Some of these missions became associated with oppression, while others focused on integration rather than imperialism.

Meanwhile, Orthodox Christianity, which since its schism from the Catholic church, had remained entrenched and resistant to change around the Patriarch's base in Constantinople, was also extending. Its expansion had been frustrated in the south by Islam and in the east by Hinduism, but the mission of its monks into Russia had been very successful. In fact, after Constantinople had been conquered by the Ottoman Turks in 1453, Christians in Moscow began to see their city as the world centre of the faith with its own Patriarch. But the church over-reached its powers in the late seventeenth century, with the result that Tsar Peter the Great abolished the office of Patriarch and made the church a department of state.

War and tolerance

As the seventeenth century mired one European country after another in war, it is clear that the political battle lines were sharpened by differences among Christians with irreconcilable theologies. For example, eight decades of tolerance for Protestants in France came to an abrupt end in 1685 when, following a royal edict, the Huguenots (French Protestants) had to convert or flee.

The terrible years of the English Civil War had their religious significance heightened by the fact that Charles I emphasized that his powers came directly from God and could not be called into account by the people. His opponent Oliver Cromwell appointed to leadership in his army Baptists and other nonconformists. Baptists were a new denomination who believed that an appropriate pattern for church life could only be found in the New Testament, notably insisting that the right moment for baptism was in adulthood. For the king to be executed was profoundly traumatic and, although the victorious Cromwell allowed a state church to continue, it was broader and there was freedom to worship in other traditions.

The restoration of the monarchy under Charles II was followed by the Act of Uniformity in 1662, which reasserted Anglicanism (the Church of England and those churches subsequently founded on its model) as the religion of England. It led to further persecution against Roman Catholics and nonconformists, including John Bunyan, who wrote the classic *Pilgrim's Progress* in Bedford Jail.

In 1688 the 'Glorious Revolution' brought the Dutch William and Mary to the English throne, and with it a certain amount of religious tolerance. One group that benefited was the Society of Friends (or Quakers) whose spiritual quest for the unvarnished power of Jesus had previously led to great suffering at the hands of the church they criticized. The tolerance did not, however, extend to Roman Catholics.

Reason and beyond

During the years when having a profound Christian belief could bring violent conflict, many lost heart. For some there grew a distinction between Christianity (a faith that involved following Jesus) and the church (the religion that formalized it). Others found themselves marginalizing religion altogether as rationalism became attractive. Depending on the part of the world, the Christian faith during the last 300 years has become either the strongest or the weakest it has ever been.

must know

• **Rationalism means the doctrine that everything humans need to know in order to discover truth can be worked out by reason, without reference to any revelation from a god.**
• **The Enlightenment is the name given to the movement in eighteenth-century Europe that used raw, logical thought to analyze all previously held doctrines. Philosophers associated with this way of thinking are John Locke, David Hume and Voltaire.**

Reason and retreat

For Europeans during the eighteenth century a new way of viewing humankind was emerging. Scientific study, which in the past had been seen as a way of revealing the magnificent purposes of God, was accelerating. Confidence was growing that with understanding would come an ability to master everything and use it for the benefit of humans. The more reason was seen to explain things, the less need there was to believe in miracles to account for the complexity of the world. It was possible to conceive of a world which had no God – or perhaps a 'watchmaker' god who had set the world in motion but never intervened from his remote distance.

For Christians, whose faith was based on a God who has come so close to humankind that he was born, died and miraculously raised to life among them, this was a profound challenge. Persuasive movements in the church began to think what shape the Christian faith would have if the miraculous and supernatural elements were excluded from it. Many felt comfortable acknowledging a Supreme Being, remote and barely knowable, but struggled with the Christian belief that, in Jesus, God had inhabited human flesh. It was possible to be a significant leader in the church while holding this 'deist' view. A group called the Unitarians, rejecting the theology of the Trinity in which Jesus is one with God, grew in popularity.

There was a genuine sense of mission in the belief that, stripped of elements that people found beyond belief, Europeans would wholeheartedly respond to the rational Christianity that was left. However, in practice the Protestant church became defensive, and, without the courage to proclaim the emotional power of Jesus' call, its ability to hold out transformation to spiritually needy people was weakened.

Revival and outreach

In Europe a refreshing wind of revival blew through the church because of preaching that began to speak to the heart. And it took place in the context of missionary activity which meant that, in a sense, Christianity could see itself for the first time as a worldwide faith.

The seeds of revival were sown in the seventeenth century in Germany, where the Pietistic movement rediscovered a warm and loving encounter with the risen Jesus. It contrasted with the hard-line, cerebral religion that some Protestant churches had come to offer. One of the Pietistic groups was the Moravian Brethren, who had a scattered and war-weary membership. It was at one of their services in London in 1738 that John Wesley had an emotional and life-changing realization of what Jesus had done for him through dying and rising.

John Wesley and his brother Charles became convinced that the people of Britain and Ireland must hear the news of salvation through Jesus Christ. They

must know

John Wesley's defining moment came at a meeting of the Moravian Brethren:

• 'I felt my heart strangely warmed. I feel I did trust in Christ, Christ alone, for salvation; an assurance was given me that he had taken away my sins, even mine, and saved me from the law of sin and death.'

began a travelling ministry and preached a dynamic message that Jesus could bring fulfilment. Despite (or perhaps because of) opposition from churches, the message preached in market places and at crossroads drew enormous crowds to declare their conversion. Faith, described with passion and made simple in hymns, became particularly attractive to working-class men and women.

The Wesleys' mission was taking place in parallel with that of other commanding preachers – George Whitefield in England and Scotland, Howell Harris in Wales and Jonathan Edwards in the United States, where a 'Great Awakening' of faith had an impact on the religious life of the nation that is still in evidence today.

Pastoral care and spiritual guidance for the large numbers of converts became a pressing issue. Within the Anglican church Wesley encouraged new believers to have a disciplined 'method' of prayer and Bible study. For mutual support they created for themselves a society nicknamed Methodists. Sadly, the Anglican Church could not adapt imaginatively enough to keep the Methodists among them and the result was a new worldwide denomination.

The 'evangelical' Christianity at the heart of this revival was deeply attractive to many poor people, who had not found churches to be welcoming places. But it was having an impact on the middle and upper classes as well. Their spiritual needs and responsibilities became the concern of a group within the Church of England called the Clapham Sect. As leading politicians and professionals (including William Wilberforce, Charles Simeon and Lord Shaftesbury), they used their influence to bring about sweeping social reforms. Among the causes to which they made substantial contributions

did you know?

The two most commonly muddled words in Christianity are 'evangelistic' and 'evangelical'.

• Evangelistic means enthusiastic to tell others the gospel and encourage them to find faith.

• Evangelical means the strand of Christian belief that stresses the importance of a personal relationship with Jesus and commitment to a life shaped by the Bible.

were the end of the trade in slaves, the regulation of working hours for children and the improvement of working conditions in mines and factories.

As Europeans continued to colonize the rest of the world, religion became one of their key exports. Protestant Christianity reached as far as the Jesuits had taken Catholicism in the previous century. Trading companies were expected to promote the faith that they had practised in their homeland – the Dutch to South Africa and present-day Sri Lanka, the British to India and the Caribbean and so on. Missionary societies were formed, funded by donations from the public. The Society for Promoting Christian Knowledge and the Society for the Propagation of the Gospel advanced education and the Bible both in Britain and abroad. Others followed, such as the Church Missionary Society and similar denominational organizations, many still in existence, reshaping themselves for the culture of succeeding generations.

must know
While revolutions in other parts of Europe in the eighteenth century were fuelled by violence, it is plausible to believe that the social revolutions in Britain that dramatically improved conditions for the most vulnerable people were fuelled by Christian faith. The Enlightenment demands that all beliefs must be based on evidence were being fulfilled in the experience of men and women whose everyday lives were being changed for the better.

Challenge and change

The importance of emotion, nature and other worldly influences was given a new respectability by the Romantic movement, shaped by philosophers such as Jean Jacques Rousseau and poets such as William Wordsworth. The Catholic church, recovering from a low point at which Pope Pius IX was forced to flee Rome in disguise, began to revive. It offered an alternative to belligerent, revolutionary atheism. Pius IX condemned nearly all modern ideas and consolidated the traditional strength of his office by calling a council at the Vatican (the tiny city-state within Rome that is the Pope's base). It pronounced the Pope to be infallible (above the possibility of criticism that he might have made a mistake) when it came to explaining matters of faith.

These influences were also evident within the Anglican church, where the Oxford Movement gained popularity alongside a cultural fascination with mediaeval times, particularly Gothic architecture. The leaders of the movement took inspiration from the clarity and courage of the mediaeval church. There was a renewed emphasis on the priest's role in communion services and God's presence in the bread and wine. This understanding of worship was much more like that of Catholicism, and one of its leaders, John Henry Newman, converted to the Roman Catholic church, where he became a cardinal.

In energetic response, Protestant leaders began new enterprises in the nineteenth century. The Brethren offered simple and non-hierarchical worship that was as different from Anglo-Catholicism as it was possible to be. The Baptist clergyman Charles Spurgeon founded a theological college and packed churches with his inspirational teaching. William Booth founded the Salvation Army in response to a need for the gospel to reach the poorest and the homeless with both practical and spiritual help. The Bible Societies and the Scripture Union were established, their evangelism focusing on the Bible and children respectively. The Church Army was founded by Wilson Carlile to train lay people to take the good news to slums where clergy dared not go.

Two major challenges prompted this activity. The Industrial Revolution brought prosperity to some, but drove an impoverished mass to the cities.

must know

The leaders of the Oxford Movement in the nineteenth century were John Keble, Edward Pusey and John Henry Newman. They issued a series of persuasive tracts (religious pamphlets), which is why it is also known as the Tractarian Movement. Their distinctive theology is still much in evidence in the Church of England in Anglo-Catholic ('high') churches, where incense, coloured vestments, candles and ornaments have an enduring significance.

And the advances of science – particularly Charles Darwin's theory of natural selection – encouraged people to examine with scepticism the parts of the Bible that described how and why the world was created.

For many Christians a more questioning approach to faith, in which there was room for doubt, was the only appropriate response. Liberal Christianity, which tended to see Jesus less as a miracle-worker and more as the outstanding human of history, was attractive to many. It made sense of science by treating the supernatural parts of the Bible as metaphors and it rose to the challenge of poverty by obeying Jesus' teaching about sacrificial living.

One inhabited world

For British Christians, overseas evangelism regained its urgency in the nineteenth century. Mission had new tools – hymn books and books of Bible stories. It also had new exponents – devoted lay people with a taste for adventure (particularly women, for whom opportunities for Christian service were limited at home). Medicine and education went hand in hand with preaching to make known the fulfilled life that Jesus could bring.

Catholic mission work renewed its energy in South and Central America. Protestant energies brought the good news (along with more controversial cultural change) to Africa and Asia. The long-term result has been that although Christianity is declining in Europe in the present day, it is dramatically growing in the countries to which the Victorian missionaries went.

must know

In bringing together evangelism, social action and stirring worship, the Salvation Army has had an impact on Christianity that exceeds its size. These words are typical of the dynamism of its founder William Booth:

• 'While women weep, as they do now, I'll fight. While little children go hungry, as they do now, I'll fight. While men go to prison, in and out, in and out, as they do now, I'll fight. While there is a drunkard left, while there is a poor lost girl upon the streets, while there remains one dark soul without the light of God, I'll fight. I'll fight to the very end!'

must know

must know

The value of the cultural change that European missionaries brought to other continents can be debated. The abolition of widow burning in India (for which the Baptist missionary William Carey campaigned) and the end of women's foot binding in China (which Gladys Aylward urged as good news) are seen as liberating influences. The imposition of particular styles of dress less so.

David Livingstone, missionary, doctor and relentless explorer, was convinced that the slave trade might revive unless there was an economic alternative and saw the development of agriculture and trade in Africa as part of the Christian gospel. However, it is now recognized that Africans themselves, such as Samuel Crowther, the first black Anglican bishop, have had the most enduring impact on Christianity in that continent.

In the United States, civil war and the freedom of the slaves had divided the population, with both sides enlisting God in their cause. The men who laid the political foundations of the secular democracy that is now familiar in US politics were largely deists. However, the denominations had more to gain than to lose from a constitutional separation of church and state. Many of them had a history of being persecuted minorities in the Europe that their predecessors left and had no desire to see one particular denomination elevated as the state church.

The most notable North American evangelist of the nineteenth century was Dwight Moody who, with the musician Ira Sankey, pioneered evangelism through huge rallies at which people were asked to make an on-the-spot commitment to follow Jesus. In the early twentieth century a new movement began to emerge in Los Angeles, where a revival was sparked by experiences that reproduced the events of the Jerusalem church in the weeks after Jesus' resurrection – speaking in tongues, healing and 'charismatic' experiences. From this modest beginning have grown the Pentecostal churches, with worship characterized by enthusiasm, joy and apparently miraculous healing in response to an invitation to God's Holy Spirit to work powerfully. The majority of the growth of the Christian church in the developing world in the present day has been through Pentecostal theology and worship.

With young churches springing up in countries that did not have centuries of Christian tradition to shape them, the leaders of the European and American churches were aware of the danger of passing on to them the divisions and controversies of other continents. Out of this determination has grown a movement toward ecumenism, with a deeply spiritual vision of the unity that Jesus longed for, and a drive to bring together denominations that have been divided, often violently, for centuries.

War and sacrifice

The optimism that human progress need have no bounds was dealt a shocking blow by the First World War. As people came to terms with the terrible suffering, many came to the end of their belief in the possibility of a loving God. Others found themselves able to see the relevance of the Christian story of human sin and godly salvation to events that had engulfed the world. The theologian Karl Barth helped revitalize Christian thought, attacking liberal Christianity and reasserting the possibility of the supernatural. He argued that the attempt to get the measure of an infinite Being was impossible, and that humans should have the humility to 'let God be God' through his revelation to the world, notably in Jesus and in the Bible. Confidence of this kind was going to become crucial for Christians as the world faced wars, the rise of totalitarianism (particularly in Nazi Germany) and godless communism in eastern Europe.

With the collapse of the tsars in Russia, as part of the Bolshevik Revolution of 1917, came a massive reaction against a church whose leadership had become completely identified with the ruling classes. The philosopher and revolutionary Karl Marx saw not only Christianity but all religion as 'an opiate of the people', which allowed the wealthy to exploit

must know

• Charismatic Christians are those who exercise 'gifts' that are granted by the Holy Spirit. While this is actually true of all Christians, who attribute their compassionate or practical skills to God, it is used particularly of those who use ecstatic words and seek miraculous events during highly charged worship.

• Ecumenism means 'one inhabited world'. Protestant, Orthodox and Pentecostal churches came together in 1948 to form the World Council of Churches. The Roman Catholic church, although not a member, is working increasingly closely with other denominations as decades go by. One expression of this was the decision of the Roman Catholic Pope and the Orthodox Patriarch in 1968 to end the excommunications that had divided them for over 1000 years.

the poor by promising better times ahead in Heaven. As communist governments attempted to establish total control over the lives of their people, the churches were treated with ruthless hostility. The 46,000 Russian churches of the beginning of the twentieth century had been reduced to a few hundred by the 1930s. For several decades Christians in communist countries chose between a life-threatening opposition to the communist regime and a compromised alliance between the church and the state.

The response of Christians to the challenge of Adolf Hitler was mixed. Most church leaders failed to see what might lie ahead as he rose to power. Some Roman Catholic leaders preached against euthanasia for disabled people and the persecution of the Jews, and paid for it dearly. Others were weak at a time when explicit opposition was called for. The Confessing Church, a Protestant denomination, held firm against the Nazis, preaching that following the way of Jesus with integrity was worthless if it could not contend with cost and challenge. For Dietrich Bonhoeffer this refusal of 'cheap grace' led to execution; for Martin Niemöller it led to a concentration camp.

must know

Dietrich Bonhoeffer was a leader of the Lutheran Church, executed in 1945 after being implicated in a plot to kill Hitler:
• 'When Christ calls a man, he bids him come and die ... Give me such love for God and for men, as will blot out all hatred and bitterness.'

Modern and postmodern

In the UK, after the Second World War, Christians played a significant role in the emergence of the Welfare State, which has made a striking impact on the health and education of vulnerable people. William Temple, a notable wartime Archbishop of Canterbury, expounded principles of human equality before God. These decades also saw the founding of major charities addressing global poverty – Oxfam growing out of the Quaker movement, Cafod from the Catholic church and

Christian Aid from the other denominations. In 1985 the Church of England report 'Faith in the City' showed the church putting itself dogmatically on the side of the poor even at the cost of antagonizing politicians; the Church Urban Fund is one of many ways in which that concern translates into practical action.

However, the last 60 years have seen a rapid decline in the number of British people who attend church. Between 1970 and 2000, church membership effectively halved. The only part of the UK to show a different trend was Northern Ireland, where the political significance associated with being either Catholic or Protestant made church attendance a defining statement. However, the more stable political engagement since the Good Friday agreement of 1998 has made the challenge faced by Irish churches more like that of the British.

Since the Second World War, archaeology has brought new excitements (notably the 1947 discovery of scrolls beside the Dead Sea, which showed Old Testament writings to be much more reliable than had been assumed). But theology has brought new confusions (notably the 1963 publication of John Robinson's doubts that there is an objective God in *Honest to God*, which showed bishops to be much less reliable than had been assumed)!

An increasingly wealthy society, seeking worth in style and consumer choice, and transcendence in sex, has been less inclined to engage with a faith that requires patience, search and sacrifice in order to reveal its enduring value. Despite that context, however, there have been notable successes. The rallies of the US evangelist Billy Graham during four decades, with their simple explanation of how a Bible-centred decision to follow Jesus can improve life and offer eternity, captured

must know
- Modernism was a trend of thought in the twentieth century that consciously broke with the past and affirmed the power of humans to improve their world through scientific, technological and artistic progress.
- Postmodernism has grown out of a sense that modernism (or any other 'ism' that attempts to define a universal truth) has failed. It encourages people to look for pathways through life that are more personal, spiritual, beautiful and aware of its complexity. This is the spirit that informs the worldview of most people in Europe and the USA.

thousands of imaginations. At the beginning of the 21st century, the very different approach of the Alpha course – using the context of food and discussion to present a version of the Christian gospel that emphasizes a personal decision to follow Jesus – has had an equal impact.

The rise of festivals such as Spring Harvest, attracting 50,000, has allowed UK Christians to regain the confidence that comes from being surrounded by a substantial body of believers. And new translations of the Bible into English have made it possible to read it in versions that are either easier to understand or closer to the original than any that had been published before.

The growing churches have been those that match contemporary culture in the vitality of their worship. In the last decades of the twentieth century the Charismatic Movement encouraged Christians to seek euphoric worship through the outpouring of the Holy Spirit. For some this meant breaking away from traditional churches to form new groupings. Originally known as house churches, because those were their usual meeting places, they now have denomination-like structures and are known as New Churches or Community Churches. And immigration has brought with it thriving and growing Black-led Churches, with a Pentecostal theology.

Growth reflecting the vigour of preaching and musicianship is also evident within the traditional Protestant denominations, where the trend is toward fewer, larger churches. The increasing prominence of women in leadership roles has brought diversity and confidence in many areas of church life – although the ordination of women in the Church of England since 1994 was painful for some who cannot share its theological rationale. The start of the twenty-first century has also seen an Emerging Church movement in the UK, which has offered a spiritual home for young Christian adults, questioning, reflecting and pursuing justice. Their worship, visually and musically at one with the culture, is inclusive and compelling, and the Greenbelt Christian Arts Festival, which draws them together, has grown five-fold since the turn of the century. They have taken advantage of all the possibilities offered by technology (a few meet only on-line, not face to face).

A world church

Throughout Christianity there has been a movement away from hierarchical churches, dominated by priests, and an understanding has grown that the whole people of God together create the church. In the Roman Catholic church this was given a huge boost by the Second Vatican Council, convened by Pope John XXIII in 1962. It marked a new engagement with culture through the introduction of worship in vernacular languages instead of Latin, new hymns and an acceptance of principles of religious tolerance.

The impact of change in the Roman Catholic church has been seen most notably in Latin America, where Christianity thrives, particularly in recent years when Catholicism has championed human rights and dignity. The most significant movement has been Liberation Theology, which suggests that the ways of God are seen most clearly when viewed through the eyes of the poor and marginalized – those who originally found hope when they met Jesus in person. It inspired a generation of priests in the 1970s to oppose repressive regimes in Central and South America, preaching courageously that the gospel of Jesus Christ announces freedom from oppression.

In the United States, Christianity is the religion embraced by most people, with 40 per cent claiming to attend (and about half that number actually attending) church regularly. The forces that have shaped it in the last 50 years have included the civil rights movement. The emergence of the pastor of a Baptist church, Martin Luther King, as its leader allowed the advances of black men and women to be shaped by a unique combination

must know

must know

• Words of Helder Camara, who as Bishop of Recife, continued to speak for the poor of South America despite criticism:
'When I give food to the poor they call me a saint. When I ask why the poor have no food they call me a communist.'
• Words of Martin Luther King, who led the civil rights movement in North America until his violent death in 1968:
'The richer we have become materially, the poorer we have become morally and spiritually. We have learnt to fly the air like birds and swim the sea like fish, but we have not yet learnt the simple art of living together like brothers.'
• Words of Desmond Tutu, Archbishop Emeritus of Cape Town and a vehement opponent of apartheid:
'Goodness is stronger than evil; love is stronger than hate; light is stronger than darkness; life is stronger than death. Victory is ours through him who loved us.'

of the challenge of Jesus to love your enemies and the unexpectedly powerful strategy of non-violence.

Today Christianity in the USA is dominated by evangelical theology. Over half a century, evangelical Christians have constructed a Christian subculture with its own schools, shops and television channels. An unyielding line on chastity outside heterosexual marriage, abortion and differentiation in the roles of men and women has had a striking impact on US politics. An extreme view of the inerrancy of the Bible, known as fundamentalism, has allowed the theory that the universe is only a few thousand years old and was created in the manner described in Genesis, to be debated as credible.

The places in which Christianity is growing apace are those where poverty is an everyday reality, or where persecution clarifies the meaning of commitment to a faith. In China, where all places of worship were closed in the decade before 1976, there may be as many as 50 million Christians. In many countries of eastern Europe, it was Protestant and Catholic churches who were able to mobilize opposition to the state as Communism began to fail in the 1980s.

In South Africa in the late twentieth century, Christians came to be identified less with the inexcusable colonial legacy that had justified apartheid and (particularly inspired by Desmond Tutu) more with opposition to discrimination based on the colour of people's skin. Throughout sub-Saharan Africa, denominational churches thrive and so do independent churches that have a strongly Pentecostal theology. These are the heirs of mass movements between 1910 and 1930 led by evangelists who had no official status in the denominations that had sent missionaries to Africa during the Victorian era. Their first, inspirational leaders (such as Sampson Oppong in Ghana, Simon Kimbangu in present-day DR Congo and Joseph Ayo Babalola in Nigeria) had scant theological education, but a much deeper understanding of African culture and spiritual need than the missionaries from Europe.

Indigenous African churches are extremely varied, and some have incorporated elements of tribal religion into their worship, but they offer a radical alternative to the hatred that drives witchcraft. As well as offering a future hope beyond death to people for whom illness and poverty (especially related to HIV) are ever present, their worship holds out tangible blessings now – miracles, ecstatic and life-affirming worship, and the strength to do God's work. This empowerment allows people with very little control over their lives a sense of personal worth, as well as a loving community.

The centre of gravity of Christianity is moving south. It is a more global religion than it has ever been. The supposed final words of Jesus to his closest followers, that they should 'be my witnesses to the ends of the earth' are literally being fulfilled in the actions of their faithful successors.

want to know more?
• *The History of Christianity*, Jonathan Hill, Lion Handbooks, 2007

6 The church in the present day

About one third of the world's population, approaching 2 billion people, call themselves Christians. Together, as followers of the way of Jesus, they make up one church. However, they are spread across many countries and cultures, and there are variations of worship and beliefs. As the Christian centuries have passed, Jesus' followers have not had a good record of accommodating each others' differences. They have preferred to distance themselves from those with whom they disagree. Today, most Christian denominations acknowledge each others' right to exist, although sometimes their members are cautious or misinformed. This chapter explains the distinctive features of the various Christian groupings.

Many denominations

Each denomination has its own structure of leadership and organization, as well as variations in belief and worship. Historically, claims about authenticity caused denominations to distance themselves from each other. However, the inspiration they find in the love and goodness of Jesus allows them all to share the title Christian.

must know

Rowan Williams, the 104th Archbishop of Canterbury, sums up the prayers of many followers of Jesus, not only in the UK but throughout the post-Christian world, as they look to the future:
• 'If there is one thing I long for above all else, it is that the years to come may see Christianity in this country able once more to capture the imagination of our culture, to draw the strongest energies of our thinking and feeling.'

Orthodox Christians

To walk into an Orthodox service is to escape from the tawdriness of everyday life and enter a place of mystical beauty. Worshippers move about in a cloud of sweet incense. The ethereal harmony of a choir rises and falls in the subdued light. In front of icons, placed around the church, worshippers pray, bow and light candles. Everyone stands and is free to move around, except for frail people who have 'gone to the wall' where there are seats. The Bible is read, and psalms and hymns chanted.

After some time, the focus of the worship centres on priests who are consecrating the eucharist, hidden behind a finely decorated screen (an iconostasis). Emerging dressed in magnificent vestments, they distribute bread and wine to the worshippers. Prayers for the world follow and, finally, the priest removes his vestments and preaches a sermon.

The Eastern 'Byzantine' Orthodox Churches (Russian, Greek and Balkan) see themselves as the most faithful keepers of the traditions established by the apostles. All other denominations have added or subtracted, they claim, but their faith and worship is authentic. Another group, the Oriental Orthodox Church, left the mainstream in the fifth century with theological disagreements. Their congregations are found in north-west Africa, Iraq, Iran and elsewhere and (being minorities in Muslim countries) are even more doggedly traditional.

For an Orthodox Christian, God is unknowable, and a living relationship with him will reveal more and more, but never all. Prayer and love are the marks of a true Christian, and so theological knowledge is in vain unless it leads to adoration of God and loving service in the community.

Roman Catholic Christians

Roman Catholics are conscious of being part of an immense church, one with worshippers the length and breadth of the world. The feature that binds the denomination together is the strong central authority of its leader, the pope, in what they hold to be an unbroken line of leaders that stretches back to Peter, who was given responsibility for the church by Jesus himself. The pope's clarifications of the teaching that has sustained the church through succeeding generations ('encyclicals' or 'papal bulls') carry authority worldwide. However, in recent decades there has also been encouragement to Catholics to read and learn from the Bible as well.

The mass is central to Catholic spirituality, with faithful people expected to attend every Sunday (or sometimes the previous evening) and at major Christian festivals. Since the 1960s, services are in vernacular languages (previously Latin had contributed to unity, but detracted from understanding). The mass is celebrated sometimes

must know

All churches have some formal members, some who worship but don't seek membership, and some who feel they belong in a loose sense but attend sporadically. So the meaning of statistics is not always clear, but these (from the *World Christian Encyclopaedia*, ed. David Barrett, OUP, 2001) give a sense of relative size. There are:
- 215 million Orthodox Christians
- 1057 million Roman Catholic Christians
- 288 million Protestant Christians
- 420 million Pentecostal Christians
- 50 million Christians who belong to churches that don't see themselves as part of a specific denomination.

must know

During the nineteenth century a group of Catholic churches in central Europe found themselves unable to accept the concept of a pope whose pronouncements were absolute ('infallible'), and broke away. These 'Old Catholics' number 6 million. Some Catholic groups in the USA and elsewhere also question traditional teaching, particularly on questions of sex and human reproduction.

with magnificent pomp – incense swirling, music soaring – and sometimes in a much simpler fashion. However, it is always an occasion for rich and colourful devotion.

Roman Catholic churches have some shared features. A series of paintings or reliefs around the walls tells the story of Jesus' last journey from condemnation to burial (or sometimes resurrection). These 'stations of the cross' are a help to worshippers who want to dwell on the significance of his death. There are usually statues of Jesus, saints, and particularly Mary (who is venerated almost as highly as her son). Roman Catholics also have a sense of how their actions enrich the experience of praying – making a sign of the cross on their body, lighting candles, humbly bowing to one knee ('genuflecting') before the bread and wine, or feeding the beads of a rosary through their fingers.

Service of the poor, pursuit of justice, devotion and duty feature robustly in Catholic spirituality – particularly in their priests, who are male and unmarried. The willingness in some parts of the world to accommodate local customs has led (helpfully) to cultural relevance, and (unhelpfully) to accusations of tolerating superstition.

Protestant Christians

The Protestant churches emerged during the turmoil of sixteenth-century Europe. Practices in the church of the time seemed to hold back the freedom of Jesus' message, and there was a rising nationalism that could not be reconciled with the controlling influence of the Roman Catholic church. When attempts to make room for this within the existing church failed, those who protested ('Protestants') founded new churches which, in various countries, emerged as four main groups:

• **Anglican churches** (sometimes called Episcopal churches) respect the Church of England as their founding church. They are to be found in many nations in which Britain was once the colonial power, or to which missionaries went in past centuries. The Archbishop of Canterbury is the 'first among equals' of many bishops, but he does not have jurisdiction in provinces outside England. Leaders in each province make their own decisions while staying in a close relationship with each other known as the 'Anglican communion'. Most Anglicans are African, which surprises those who picture worshippers kneeling in an English parish church.

Their beliefs are shaped by John Calvin, who insisted that the Bible should be the only authority, and that the church should add no other burdens to people's relationship with Jesus. Their practices are shaped by Martin Luther, who permitted traditions such as liturgies (set orders of service), vestments and significant furnishings, but only if they were in keeping with New Testament teaching.

These beliefs and practices were defined in the 39 Articles of Religion (in 1563) and the *Book of Common Prayer* (in 1662). Over time, the denomination has developed an ability to hold together people with extremely divergent views of doctrine and expressions of worship (although that tolerance has been and is sorely tried). This means that the experience of going to an Anglican church can be markedly different in neighbouring towns, let alone neighbouring continents. The churches share

must know

These figures suggest the relative sizes of Protestant churches. There are:
• 80 million Anglican Christians
• 50 million Lutheran Christians, 24 million Reformed Christians, and a further 25 million in churches born from uniting the two traditions
• 44 million Baptist Christians
• 15 million Methodist Christians
• 50 million Christians who belong to smaller groupings such as the Brethren (2.9 million), the Salvation Army (2.6 million), or the Quakers (0.3 million).

a prayer book, but its orders of service might be followed precisely and solemnly or loosely and joyously. They share the importance of Bible teaching and communion, but this might happen in a context of musical splendour or quiet simplicity. They share the desire to influence society for good, but whether that happens through representation on local and national bodies or through discreet neighbourliness varies from setting to setting.

• **Lutheran churches** were emerging in Scandinavia and Germany at the same time as Anglicanism. Martin Luther's influence is still evident in their worship. Hymns, liturgy and communion take place with a restrained dignity. Their priests and bishops have an exceptionally thorough training in theology, evident in their preaching with its strong emphasis on the authority of the Bible and the place of grace in reuniting humans with God. Lutherans have modelled and encouraged unity and co-operation across denominational differences ('ecumenism').

• **Reformed churches** are often known as Presbyterian churches. They are strong in Holland and Switzerland, and the Church of Scotland – the most prominent expression of Christianity in that country – belongs in this group. John Calvin, the originator of this stream of Protestantism, was even more radical than Luther in rejecting the practices of the Roman Catholic church during the sixteenth century. His very exalted view of the Bible led him to reject bishops, church decorations and most rituals (even music). His influence is still evident in the sober form of Christianity of Reformed churches, with their profound spirituality, simple worship and commitment to integrity in their involvement in business and the professions. Worship in the Church of Scotland features hymns and prayers led by a minister, building toward a sermon. Communion is infrequent, allowing for serious preparation to underline its significance.

It is within the Lutheran and Presbyterian streams of Christianity that the urge toward unity has led most clearly to action. Throughout the world there are United Lutheran and Reformed Churches. And in the last few decades, the Uniting Church in Australia and the United Reformed Church in the UK have shown the willingness of congregations to reverse the trend toward division that has marred the Christian centuries.

• **Baptist churches** emerged in the same century in response to a sense that what it meant to be a true Christian had been replaced by lifestyles that bore the name of Christianity, but did not have a committed integrity. It seemed to the founders of the Baptist movement that because virtually everyone was baptized as a baby, it had ceased to hold significance as a witness to a decision to follow Jesus. Baptists then and now baptize believers in adulthood instead, immersing them completely under water.

Baptists are 'congregational' in nature, which means that their direction is set by the entire congregation through elections and shared decision-making. This makes Baptist churches remarkably varied. However, a love of the Bible and a sense of urgency about evangelism characterize life in Baptist congregations. They are strong (and distinctly conservative) in states in the south of the

must know

In contexts where Christians are few, denominational differences decrease in significance (particularly between Protestant churches). This is especially true of places where mission is recognized as imperative. And in the UK, where consumer choice drives much of society, people coming to the Christian faith with little knowledge of its history increasingly regard denomination as a matter of personal preference for style of worship, time or location.

USA, and also in countries to which Baptist missionaries first went, such as India. Typically, they worship with an absence of ritual but a strong sense of needing to make a response of faith and service. There is sung praise, prayer, preaching and communion. As well as these four Protestant groups there are smaller denominations, some of which have had a significance that considerably exceeds their size. Among them are:

- **Methodist churches**, which followed the lead of John and Charles Wesley in the eighteenth century. Their methodical approach to faith and life was never intended to create a new denomination, but Anglicanism could not contain it. With no bishops in the UK, but a strong involvement of lay people (those who are not ordained as clergy), Methodism has made a distinctive contribution to Christian life. Methodist worship has always featured a love of hymn-singing and simple liturgy. An annual covenant service allows believers to offer themselves wholeheartedly to God's service: 'I am no longer my own but yours ... Let me be full, let me be empty; let me have all things, let me have nothing; I freely and wholeheartedly yield all things to your pleasure and disposal.'

- **The Salvation Army, the Brethren** and **the Quakers** are other denominations picked from a long list of Protestant denominations. The uniformed Salvation Army has strong traditions in social action among the most vulnerable in society, evangelism wherever the need is greatest and fine music-making. The Brethren, with no clergy, no symbols, no instruments, but a love of the Bible and communion, have a (male-dominated and sometimes exclusive) commitment to shared worship and shared life. Quakers (to give its full title, the Religious Society of Friends) have made silence central to their gatherings since the seventeenth century, with anyone allowed to break the stillness and share thoughts inspired by the Holy Spirit. Rejecting creeds in favour of an ongoing search for the light of God, their record of pacifism and peace-making has distinguished them among Christian denominations.

Pentecostal Christians

Considering their history stretches back little more than a century, Pentecostal churches have seen a remarkable expansion, and their growth is set to continue (particularly in Africa, Asia and Latin America). The congregations are attractive to join because they offer warm and supportive friendship.

Pentecost was the occasion, during the year of Jesus' resurrection, when his followers found themselves captivated by the Holy Spirit. It was so overwhelming that they spoke in languages previously unknown to them, found the ability to bring healing from God to people and became fervently motivated to spread the good news of Jesus. All those things still happen during Pentecostal worship. It is extremely lively, charged with emotion, and to some extent unplanned, with members of the congregation singing in euphoric languages, praying for each other, and bringing messages directly from God.

These 'gifts of the Spirit' are used to encourage and challenge the congregation. 'Speaking in tongues' is the ecstatic language used in praise of

must know

Several Pentecostal denominations have now had time to establish themselves with organizational structures, such as the Elim Pentecostal Church and the Assemblies of God (whose Yoido Full Gospel Church in South Korea is the world's largest congregation – about 800,000). However, because Pentecostal theology values obedience to the direction of the Holy Spirit above any human administrative system, independent churches broadly within this tradition spring up without reference to denominational planning.

Often the new congregation grows out of an adverse reaction to inhibiting traditions of an existing church. In Africa and Asia they are flourishing under indigenous leadership and, freed from Western missionary conventions, are responding to pressing local needs. In the UK a large number of churches were created during the 1970s, making room for the exuberant spiritual experiences that seemed absent in traditional churches. Initially called 'house churches', because that is where the small groups of Christians met, many have thrived to such an extent that they own properties and have denomination-like networks.

God, sometimes chanted by many people in exuberant harmony and sometimes spoken by one person with another 'translating' it into the local language.

'Ministry' is a period during which the Spirit, in a way that is unpredictable, works through people's prayers to bring healing, laughter, tears, intense relaxation or assurance of God's care.

'Prophecy' is a short message believed to be given by the Holy Spirit, addressed to an individual, a congregation or even a whole nation. It usually makes a theme of the Bible directly relevant to present circumstances.

All these features follow singing of a more conventional kind and a high-powered sermon that expounds the Bible. Pentecostal Christians are conscious of offering their whole bodies in praise of God during worship, when arms raised in praise of God or hands held open as if to receive a blessing are a familiar sight.

The theology of Pentecostal churches stresses conversion, through repentance and belief in Jesus, as the point of salvation. For some, 'baptism in the Spirit' is a secondary experience in which power to be a Christian witness is received, and its coming is signalled by the ability to speak in tongues. Forthright teaching by leaders who are held in high esteem has the benefit of engendering hope and purpose, but has sometimes attracted criticism for being overbearing.

A world church

Among Jesus' final exhortations to his followers was that they should make people throughout every nation of the world his disciples. The devotion with which they have done this has had spectacular results worldwide. However, Jesus also prayed during his final days that his followers would be united. Coming to a common mind about what it means to be a faithful Christian has proved more elusive.

Many traditions

The Christian faith throughout the world is distinguished by a belief in God the Trinity. This 'Trinitarian' belief holds together virtually all those who identify themselves as Christians. However, with so many adherents, it is not surprising that there are differences of emphasis in the way believers grasp their theology. Five streams of thinking overlap each other and cross many borders. Across the nations and denominations can be found Christians holding dear (and sometimes arguing over) these ways of approaching their faith:

• **Evangelical Christians** hold a personal relationship with the risen Jesus to be vital to a meaningful Christian faith, and stress the importance of the Bible in showing the right way to live. Worship that is low on ceremonial and high on excitement has made this strand of Christian practice accessible to those without much religious experience, and young people find it engaging. Conversion, commitment and

must know

George MacLeod, a Scottish Presbyterian minister and founder of a community that has made the island of Iona a centre of Christian hope once more:

• 'The living church, though never neat, keeps the world from complete disaster.'

witness in the community feature strongly. Sometimes evangelical Christians place themselves on a scale from 'conservative' to 'open', depending on their willingness to engage with the changing mores of society. But they stand apart from fundamentalists, who insist on a literal interpretation of the Bible.

• **Liberal Christians** question the Christian tradition they have inherited. Their sincere respect for the Bible acknowledges the context in which it was written, including the cultural circumstances that constrained writers to have particular moral views and the limited scientific understanding that fostered a belief in supernatural miracles. For example, the inspiration of the risen Jesus in the present is a more significant truth than whether the historical Jesus rose from death in a physical body. They stress that the Holy Spirit of God is working in each generation in a new way, leading Christians to frame new ethical responses to the world's issues (challenging global injustice features strongly; dictating personal sexual morality less so).

• **Anglo-Catholic Christians** (particularly in the Anglican Church) have a very high regard for the church – its sacraments, its priesthood and its history. Often conservative in their interpretation of the Bible, they are deeply respectful of the tradition they have inherited and the saintly people who have shaped the Christian faith through the centuries. Anglo-Catholics use words carefully and reverently when it comes to describing God, but also know when to be silent in the face of his wonder and mystery. This results in worship that is high on sensory experience, with colourful vestments (rich in

---

must know

Teresa of Avila, a sixteenth-century nun from Spain:
• 'Christ has no body now on earth but yours, no hands but yours, no feet but yours. Yours are the eyes through which look out Christ's compassion for the world; yours are the feet on which he is to go about doing good; yours are the hands with which he is to bless men now.'

symbolism), incense, bells, ritual movements and a profound reverence for the bread and wine of the eucharist.

• **Charismatic theology** has influenced all three of those strands during the last 40 years. Sometimes it is described as 'the renewal movement'. Charismatic worship takes the features of Pentecostal churches associated with the coming of the Holy Spirit into the liturgies of all the other denominations. This desire to let the Holy Spirit enrich and direct lives has occasionally divided churches, where some are suspicious of its emotional thrill.

• **Liberation theology** is a movement which started in Latin America that has politicized some Roman Catholic churches in poor communities. Inspired by God's leading of his people out of oppression into freedom, it urges all Christians to stand alongside poor people in their pursuit of justice. It sees salvation as overturning the sins inherent in the structures of society, more than repenting of personal sins. This is how the gospel of Jesus impacts on those whose experience of life is primarily being sinned against, rather than being sinners. Its influence has spread through Protestant churches, both rich and poor, but particularly where 'base communities' in shanty towns study the Bible, pray and together take practical action ('praxis').

Many faiths

There has never been a time when Christianity was the sole religion of the world, and the way Christians relate to those of other faiths continues to be a matter of concern in this generation. Three different

must know

Hildegard of Bingen, a twelfth-century German nun and composer:
• 'Be not lax in celebrating. Be not lazy in the festive service of God. Be ablaze with enthusiasm. Let us be an alive, burning offering before the altar of God.'

must know

Thomas Carlyle,
nineteenth-century
Scottish historian:
• 'If Jesus Christ were to
come today, people would
not crucify him. They
would ask him to dinner,
and hear what he had to
say, and make fun of it.'

ways that theologians understand the relationship
are as follows:

• **An exclusive approach** suggests that only those
who believe Jesus to be God will have eternal
salvation. This approach engenders urgent
missionary activity out of love for people who might
lose their place in Heaven because they follow a
non-Christian religion.

• **An inclusive approach** suggests that the
salvation that Jesus brought to humankind is
sufficient for everyone, whether they realize it or not.
So no matter what shortcomings non-Christian
religions may have, they still bring the saving grace
of God to their believers.

• **A pluralist approach** puts God, rather than Jesus,
at the centre of faith, and suggests that all religions
lead to the same God. For those Christians who are
persuaded by this approach it is a joy to seek
common ground with those of other religious
convictions.

Mission

The fact that Christians are not agreed among
themselves about the status of other religions serves
only to increase the difficulty of conversation with
those who do not share their core beliefs. Missionary
societies continue to send men and women from
predominantly Christian countries into the
developing world. Most societies encourage people
with skills of which there is a shortage in the
developing world (for instance, teaching, medicine or
agriculture) to work on projects that bring tangible
improvements to the quality of life of poor people.

Because they are driven to do this by the compassion of God, it is hoped that those who benefit from their work will respond with gratitude to and curiosity about Jesus. However, societies for whom an exclusive attitude is compelling also send missionaries to found churches in countries where Christianity is a minority faith, with the specific intention of urging people to change their religion ('proselytizing').

Groups loosely associated with Christianity

There are a number of groups that share some of the tenets of Christianity, but have idiosyncratic beliefs that place them outside the mainstream of the faith. These include Mormons (the Church of Jesus Christ of the Latter Day Saints), Jehovah's Witnesses, Christian Scientists and Spiritualists.

Although their convictions and practices are diverse, in each case, a charismatic leader during the nineteenth century claimed to have had a revelation from God that added to or clarified the teaching of the Bible. Beliefs about life and eternity which are mysterious in the Bible were made specific, and have become as significant in the groups' dogma as the teaching of Jesus. These groups have clearly enriched the lives of many people, and together they number 26 million, but they are not recognized as part of the Christian mainstream.

want to know more?

• *How to Read a Church*, Richard Taylor, Rider, 2003
• www.findachurch. co.uk

7 A Christian heritage

Some of the most beautiful sights and sounds of the last 20 centuries have taken their inspiration directly from the Christian faith. However, there has always been a tension between Christians who see creativity as integral to all humans because they are in the image of the creator God, and those who are concerned that art turns people's attention from the true, divine beauty. This chapter examines how Christianity has shaped the words and music, buildings and art that are the foundations of the culture of many countries, particularly in the developed world.

Architecture and art

Jesus' ministry mostly took place out of doors. His first followers copied this, or met in each others' homes. Three hundred years later the Christian church was developing an organization that relied on identifiable buildings. And 1000 years later buildings for worship were the most spectacular and ornately decorated structures that anyone could conceive or construct.

Buildings for worship

The earliest Christian building of which traces still remain is a house in Syria that was adapted to contain a pool in which baptisms could take place and a room in which communion meals could be eaten. This dates to the third century, although before that Christians are known to have gathered for worship and commemoration of martyrs in underground burial chambers (catacombs). In times of persecution these were places of relative safety for Christians to pray. This is the first association of church with a burial place – something that is so familiar in English village churchyards that it now seems timeless.

When it became an officially recognized religion in the fourth century, church buildings were required, and Christians copied styles that were popular in the Roman empire. The basilica was a large rectangular room in which two rows of pillars gave the impression of three long, thin sections. Thousands of churches still have this pattern – a central seating area called the nave, with aisles either side. At the front of the basilica was a smaller, separate section (sometimes semi-circular) called an apse. When a service took place this became the logical place for the bishop and priests to sit and for the table bearing bread and wine (an altar) to be placed, with the other worshippers in the main part of the building. This arrangement had an impact on the style of the service – it distanced the leaders from the worshippers and introduced a theatrical formality. In countless churches today, though, it seems like the natural order of things; the priests and choir sit close to the altar at the front of a church (the chancel) in an area which is distinct from that in which the congregation worships.

Another typically Roman building that influenced Christian architecture is the round or octagonal mausoleum. This structure allowed Christians to gather

Christian practices

As centuries have gone by, Christian practices that originally developed because they were usual behaviour in ancient cultures have taken on a theological significance. For example, the two rooms in which priests and congregations worshipped because Roman architecture lent itself to this became so established that mediaeval churches in the West were constructed with elaborately carved lattices (rood screens) between the two. And the robes that some clergy wear to conduct worship relate to the tunics of Roman antiquity. Even bells, incense and candles have a history in which practical use and symbolism go hand in hand.

For some Christians, the theological meaning of these practices is imperative and their preservation has become very important (for example, a priest's position, facing toward or away from the congregation, speaks of his unique calling to represent God to people, or people to God). For others, aware of the difficulty that ordinary people have in comprehending religious customs, the need to remove cultural barriers has proved more compelling (creating churches in which those leading worship have no special uniform and the communion table is in the heart of the congregation).

round the tomb of a martyr, continuing the importance given to this in the catacombs. This round shape, topped with a dome, has become the most familiar structure for a church in the Eastern Orthodox tradition.

During the Middle Ages, the majority of churches were built of timber and were modest in character. Few have survived. However, as trade and towns expanded, churches became increasingly magnificent as an expression of civic pride. Wealthy patrons sponsored stone churches. This 'romanesque' architecture was solid, sturdy and had rounded arches. Very often the church was the most notable building for miles around and in the case of cathedrals, a marvel of engineering to honour a marvellous God.

Features of every church were an altar or table, a lectern from which the Bible was read or expounded, a throne for the bishop and a font (a great basin for water) near the entrance to indicate that it is through baptism that believers enter the church. There were no seats for the congregation. Larger churches added side chapels, with their own altar, in which relics of saints or the founders of the local church could be venerated. Gothic church architecture (from the twelfth to the sixteenth centuries) had lofty, pointed arches and sometimes the floor plan formed the shape of a cross. Stained glass filled the space with colour and provided pictures as visual aids for teaching.

The new theology of the Reformation brought new architecture. Instead of drawing attention to the distinctive powers of priests (central to Roman Catholic and Orthodox theology), it reflected the conviction that all believers are, in a sense, priests. Side altars were swept away and replaced by a moveable table that allowed everyone to worship in the same room, and a pulpit was positioned so that everyone could hear and understand from where they were sitting in pews (hence the name 'auditory church').

The emphasis of these churches was classical simplicity, but the Roman Catholic churches built in southern Europe at the time could hardly be a greater contrast, with a Baroque style of dazzling canopies and elaborately decorated columns. Protestant missionaries exported Classical simplicity to the churches they founded in the New World; Catholic missionaries exported Baroque grandeur to South America. And in Russia, Orthodox congregations were developing their own distinctive architecture, standing to worship under a hemispherical ceiling on top of which is a coloured onion dome – practical (to keep snow off) or symbolic (resembling a candle) according to different theories.

The nineteenth-century fascination in Britain with all things mediaeval led to a revival in impressive buildings whose pinnacles and traceries looked Gothic. This was a reflection of the prestige of Christianity in that era, but the splendour of the buildings was not always suitable for the activity that it housed. The simpler, inclusive structures of Methodist and Baptist congregations of the period have proved more adaptable. British church architects in the twentieth and twenty-first centuries have had the task of modifying old buildings to meet the needs of contemporary congregations. In contrast, 'megachurches' in North America and Asia have purpose-built buildings in amphitheatre style that can seat many thousands of worshippers.

Most new congregations today opt for simpler and cheaper buildings or multi-purpose rooms that can meet the varied needs of a community from Monday to Saturday and adapt for worship when it is required. Many choose not to own a building at all, but to rent space when it is required in a local school or leisure centre. At the same time churches that were built in a more expansive era but have no congregation to worship in them are being sold and adapted for commercial use. However, for many people (even those who never use it) a church building is a symbol of security in a rapidly changing world. Whether it is recognized by a steeple, an onion dome or an ornate cross, the presence of a sacred building establishes a site as having a place in the unfolding story of God's dealings with his people, and their desire to create something beautiful in appreciation of his grace.

Examples of architectural styles

See fine examples of:
- a church in the style of a Roman mausoleum in Jerusalem, where in the fourth century Constantine built a huge octagonal building around the probable site of Jesus' burial.
- a church in the style of a Roman basilica in Bethlehem, where the church above the supposed cave of Jesus' birth dates from the sixth century.
- a timber church – Urnes stave church in Luster, Norway, which dates from 1130
- Romanesque architecture in Durham, north England, where the cathedral has towered over the city since the twelfth century
- Gothic architecture – Notre Dame Cathedral – in Paris, which was completed in 1345
- an auditory church – St Clement Danes – in London, one of the churches designed by Christopher Wren after the Great Fire of London
- a Baroque church – St Peter's Basilica – in Rome, designed by Michelangelo and others
- Russian Orthodox architecture – St Basil's Cathedral, with its familiar domes – in Red Square, Moscow
- Gothic Revival architecture – St Patrick's Cathedral, New York – dedicated in 1879
- a twenty-first-century worship centre – the vast Yoido Full Gospel Church – in South Korea.

Art

From Christianity's earliest days artists had three purposes: to educate, to decorate and to glorify God through their creativity. The catacomb chambers in Rome are decorated with paintings that depict Jesus as the Good Shepherd and as a King. They show how artists dealt with their most fundamental challenge – expressing in a visible form the nature of an invisible God. They showed Jesus, God born as a human being. However, they did not represent him literally (Jesus was neither a shepherd nor a king) but symbolically.

From the fourth century to the nineteenth century Christianity was the principle reference point of art in Europe. Byzantine Orthodox Christians developed icons specifically for use in prayer. They are stylized paintings on wood of Jesus or a saint, still and intense. They were (and are) painted according to strict devotional and artistic rules that mark out their creation as an act of worship. Both created and used in prayer, they not only represent, but embody the subject as they are revered.

The huge mosaics of fifth-century churches also represent Jesus or Mary holding him as an infant, glorious on a gold background. Haloes of light around the head distinguish Jesus and the disciples from the crowds – a symbol that persisted for a thousand years, even when advanced techniques allowed subtler characterization.

In the Europe of the Middle Ages the church was the only patron of the arts, so almost all large-scale art was essentially Christian. Thus embroiderers fashioned vestments for priests, jewellers crafted vessels for eucharist, stonemasons produced bosses for church pillars, painters created epic murals on church walls and glaziers stained glass to fill their windows. And in the

must know

The great art forms that have developed since the harnessing of electricity have engaged with Christianity in different ways. On film the story of Jesus has been told more than twenty times since DW Griffiths' silent epic *Intolerance* in 1916. The most successful is usually considered to be Pier Paulo Pasolini's still and meditative *The Gospel According to St Matthew* in 1964. People of faith have generally been presented more sympathetically on film than they have during the same century in novels, from William Wyler's 1959 *Ben-Hur* (in which an encounter with Jesus creates a compassion that is stronger than revenge) to Roland Joffé's 1986 *The Mission* (a morally complex story of the personal and cultural change brought by Christianity as Latin America is colonized by Europeans during the eighteenth century).

monasteries, copies of the Scriptures were made, beautifully written and spectacularly illustrated ('illuminated') with abstract decoration and pictures of the events described.

All these artefacts drew attention to the divine glory of Jesus. However, as plague swept across the nations a new subject for devotion emerged, and artists were commissioned to depict the crucified Jesus, suffering alongside his beloved followers and thus understanding their plight. In particular, paintings of the crucifixion were placed above altars where bread and wine were consecrated, so that worshippers made a connection between the pity of the dying Jesus and the life-giving eucharist that was held out to them as they knelt at the foot of his cross.

Alongside this joy in creativity has always existed a suspicion that art is subversive. It might encourage Christians to worship the object or the artist instead of God the Creator. Occasionally there have been times when this has swelled into destructive movements. In the ninth century 'iconoclasts' in the Orthodox church smashed icons and attacked their artists. And in the sixteenth century, with the Reformation taking hold, extremists destroyed church paintings and beheaded statues, dismayed that such images were idols. Instead, they decorated the churches they built with words, such as the Lord's Prayer and the Ten Commandments.

As power and wealth moved away from the church to the aristocracy during the seventeenth century, the range of subjects depicted in art diversified. Landscape, portraiture, and everyday life moved from the periphery of religious paintings to become the main subject of secular ones. The rise of abstraction in the twentieth century and conceptual art in the twenty-first have reintroduced into art a spiritual dimension, although not a specifically Christian one. Christians creating such work in Europe and the USA are often anticipating that it will be viewed in a gallery rather than a church. They respond to the centuries-old challenge of allowing an invisible God to be seen by creating work that alludes to or inspires faith, rather than portraying events described in the Bible. However, in churches worldwide creative Christians continue to produce art on a smaller scale in the tradition of education, devotion and glorification of God – banner making, flower arranging, website development. Kitsch using Christian imagery – highly sentimental and with low artistic standards – has flourished with the rise of consumerism.

Meanwhile, in the developing world a thriving tradition of painting and sculpting Christian themes endures. It follows the precedent of European art by depicting Jesus in the costume and setting of the place in which the artist lives, rather than first-century Galilee. So while Italian artists of the sixteenth century painted a caucasian Jesus in the green Umbrian hills, today's African artists may paint him as a revered tribal chief, Asian artists as a guru and Central American artists as a revolutionary.

Examples of Christian art

See fine examples of:
- fifth-century mosaics of Jesus – the Hagia Sophia Church in Istanbul
- eighth-century illuminated manuscripts – the Lindisfarne Gospels in the British Library, London
- twelfth-century icons – the Virgin of Vladimir, in the Tretyakov Gallery, Moscow
- thirteenth-century stained glass – the deep blue light that floods Chartres Cathedral, France
- fifteenth-century devotional art – the triumphant Jesus, newly raised from the dead among the trees of San Sepulcro, Italy, where it was painted by Piero della Francesca
- twentieth-century painting that refers to the traditions of Christian art – Chris Ofili's *The Upper Room* in Tate Britain, London, where thirteen paintings of monkeys are displayed in a setting like a chapel
- Christian art in the developing world – the statue of Christ the Redeemer, towering over Rio de Janeiro

Music and literature

It is impossible to understand the music and literature of Western civilization during the last thousand years without reference to Christianity, because both have been shaped by the need to express and understand faith.

Western music

Christianity is a singing religion, as was Judaism before it. One hundred and fifty songs from Jewish worship are collected in the Old Testament – psalms that allow men and women to express to God their praise, doubt, trust and anger. They were sung by Jesus, by the first Christians and, in styles that fit the local culture, by every generation of believers to this day. Very soon after the resurrection of Jesus, new songs were being written by his followers which allowed them to worship him as God. Paul, evidently a music lover, quoted from them in his letters, so they are preserved in the New Testament.

Because musical notation as we know it was not written down for the first thousand years after the life of Jesus, little record has survived. However, it is known to have favoured single-line chants, without instruments, echoing through lofty monastic spaces. The twelfth-century nun Hildegard of Bingen was a composer whose music has endured. Pure and melodic, this is the style of music from which the folk tradition of Europe has taken inspiration through the centuries.

The biggest development in Western music was the emergence in the thirteenth century of polyphony – two or more lines of music sung or played at the same time and working together to create a harmonious sound. This advance was taking place in secular and Christian music at the same time, but it was in the monasteries that a way of writing the music down developed so that a choir could sing music that had been written hundreds of miles away even though they had never heard it. Every backing singer who sings harmonies in a rock band today is, without realizing it, a descendent of this tradition (although the musical thirds and sixths that sound pleasant today are different from the fourths and fifths that would have reminded mediaeval singers of heavenly harmony).

The great flowering of church music, however, was between the sixteenth and eighteenth centuries, when the aristocracy of Europe were patrons of the arts and sustained composers, choirs and orchestras. Sacred and secular music at this time were cross-fertilizing each other. Opera was the new and seductive secular force. Christian music grew increasingly complex to maintain an equal impact, with breathtaking choral and orchestral interplay setting biblical words to rich melodies. From Thomas Tallis, writing exclusively religious music for the queen of England, to Joseph Haydn, writing Christian oratorios and secular symphonies with equal confidence for Austria's fabulously wealthy Eszterházy family, this music still dominates the programmes of the world's concert halls. However, the peak is generally regarded as having been reached by Johann Sebastian Bach whose organ music, cantatas for the church year, and musical accounts of Jesus' last days were written for the Lutheran church. He wrote 'To God alone be glory' at the foot of each manuscript, and his work conveys a sense that he was as much an awestruck worshipper as a performer.

Hymns

Martin Luther had encouraged congregational singing instead of performance by experts as one of the principles of the Reformation. This consisted mainly of chanted settings of psalms, but Luther also put Christian words to secular tunes, which opened possibilities that were to impact markedly on the way God was praised in local churches. A major issue was the insistence that the words should be heard and understood, as well as the music being beautiful. Singing in vernacular languages meant that ordinary people could join in, not just listen. Books of hymns appeared, adapting psalms from the

must know

A hymn of Isaac Watts that has retained its popularity for 300 years:

'When I survey the wondrous cross
On which the Prince of glory died,
My richest gain I count but loss,
And pour contempt on all my pride.

Were the whole realm of nature mine,
That were an offering far too small;
Love so amazing, so divine,
Demands my soul, my life, my all.'

Bible. In the eighteenth century, Isaac Watts created new possibilities by publishing a book of hymns that used his own words, rather than those paraphrased from the Bible, and some remain popular today. He prepared the ground in which many hymn writers could flourish, and Charles and John Wesley, whose hymns have a tuneful note of energetic praise, set the standard to which all congregational songwriters subsequently aspire.

The European missionaries to the developing world took their favourite hymns with them, with the result that it is possible to visit churches in Asia or South America and sing the same tunes as congregations in England. There are notable exceptions, where indigenous Christians have worked to develop a culturally distinct style of praise to God, including the rich, swooping, a capella hymns of Africa. The most obvious exception is the spiritual (formerly referred to as the negro spiritual), which has its roots in the yearning for liberation of black slaves in the USA. The intricate, multi-part harmonies, sometimes lyrical, sometimes ecstatic, accompanied words that alluded to the freedom of God's people from slavery in the Old Testament. In the early twentieth century these songs had a profound influence on gospel music, which developed such a strong following in the USA that today there are specialized radio stations which play nothing else. Gospel music in turn became the source for rock and roll, which in the second half of the twentieth century became the inspiration for almost all popular music today.

Ironically, it is now the turn of pop music to feed its influences back into church music. There is a thriving culture of new Christian music created by bands using electronic instruments, released commercially to the public on albums, and then introduced into churches to be sung by congregations. Just as in Victorian times, the quality of the writing varies enormously and time will reveal which songs have an enduring value.

Alongside this, a tradition of hymn writing in the Celtic folk tradition has re-emerged, and there has been a revival of repetitive chanting, in Latin or English, through which international groups of Christians can unite in song. And music written explicitly to move listeners to adoration of God has revived as part of the classical tradition, with John Tavener and James MacMillan creating works through which 2000 years of influence echo.

Literature

For the first few centuries of Christianity almost all Europeans sufficiently educated to write were Christians, their subject was theology and their language was Latin. In the seventh century, whether they were writing history (such as the Northumbrian monk Bede) or poetry (the farmer-poet Caedmon, writing innovatively in English) the Christian God was their theme. Even Geoffrey Chaucer in the thirteenth century, whose *Canterbury Tales* have room for chivalry and smut side by side, writes with Christian assumptions implicit as pilgrims make their way to Thomas Becket's tomb.

The influence of the Christian faith on literature is particularly clear in drama. The fine Greek and Roman traditions of drama predate Jesus, but had ended in sleazy disrepute. In eleventh-century

did you know?

Christianity's influence on television and radio has been intense since the foundation of the BBC. A legal requirement in its charter to programme a certain amount of religious broadcasting still stands, meaning that acts of worship, documentaries and drama of Christian interest have always been part of mainstream television and radio output in the UK. Broadcasting in the USA and the developing world, driven by commercial interests, has no such constraint. The result has been the rise of niche stations catering for a Christian audience, a trend that has increased with the development of internet broadcasting. Evangelists have used the opportunity this brings to generate huge television congregations for their message, but a series of scandals has made this a controversial business.

England, theatre that is recognizable as the basis of today's practice incubated in church liturgies, where parts of the life of Jesus were told in dialogue. Between the thirteenth and fifteenth centuries, these 'tropes' developed and spilled out on to the streets, where over the course of an entire day 'mystery plays' told the story of salvation from Adam and Eve to the Day of Judgement. These vivid plays employed humour, pathos and special effects to create the combination of entertainment and meaning that has been vital to theatre ever since.

The great era of European drama that followed, with Shakespeare writing in England, then the Spanish 'golden age' and the great French tragedies, saw the imagination breaking free of Christian dogma, but still the Christian view of the universe was providing the moral backdrop against which they were written. Shakespeare's last plays, *The Tempest* and *A Winter's Tale*, are stories of grace breaking through and redeeming families fractured by sin – explicitly Christian themes, although never mentioning the name of Jesus.

The 1611 publication of the Bible in an English translation of translucent beauty – the *King James (or 'Authorized') Version* – had a profound impact on subsequent literature, because its phrases and cadences have passed into the language in ways so pervasive that they are barely noticed. They impacted on those who wrote with explicitly Christian intentions from John Milton's seventeenth-century exploration of the relationship between God and humanity in *Paradise Lost* to TS Eliot's twentieth-century meditation on time and eternity, *Four Quartets*. But they also impacted on those whose subject was faith's absence, such as the Victorian poet Matthew Arnold who, in *Dover Beach*, observed 'its melancholy, long, withdrawing roar'.

For the past 200 years writers interested in the spirituality of their characters have had to deal with the fact that the decline of Christianity has not brought with it an end to guilt, restlessness or the search for some kind of salvation. For Fyodor Dostoevsky, writing as a Christian, the longing for redemption was a journey through suffering and love. For Samuel Beckett, writing as an atheist, Christianity was a memory for characters trying to hold back despair. However, it is a sign of the spiritually ambivalent times that Dan Brown's *The da Vinci Code*, while not a work of great literary quality, uses the fiction of an untrustworthy church suppressing secrets about Jesus to keep the pages turning.

There is a vigorous tradition of opposition by Christians to art that offends them, which has mistakenly given some the impression that Christianity is fundamentally anti-culture. It is usually portrayals of Jesus that do not afford him the same reverence as the Gospels that provokes campaigners to accusations of blasphemy. Religion and sex have often proved a confrontational combination. In seventeenth-century England the Puritans succeeded in having all theatres closed for eighteen years, but during the past 50 years the presence of Christian protestors has been more likely to boost the audience for a work of art.

want to know more?

• *The Christian Tradition in English Literature*, Paul Cavill and Heather Ward, Zondervan, 2007
• *Seeing Salvation*, Neil MacGregor and Erika Langmuir, BBC Books, 2000
• *Seeing Salvation*, various composers, Metronome, 2000

8 A Christian worldview

Christians have an overwhelming loyalty to the God whose Kingdom is outside time. Moral decisions need to be made about how to live together on a small planet, and for the Christian this means trying to relate the perfect love and justice of God's Kingdom to the imperfect circumstances of the world around them. For most of the last 20 centuries, Christian theology has set the standard by which, whether they liked it or not, vast numbers of people have lived. This chapter is about what it means to have a Christian worldview, and about what happens when Christians cannot agree on what it means – in practice – to live by the values of God's Kingdom.

Christian morality

As individuals we make moral choices every day. As a society we set a moral framework that ensures people are able to thrive without damaging others in the process. Christians want these things to take place in the context of belief in a God who upholds absolute standards of love and justice.

must know

Over time, a method of theological reflection has developed to help Christians discern the will of God as new moral questions arise. John Wesley is credited with first suggesting it. It holds together:
• Scripture (the Bible)
• Tradition (the history of God's action in the world)
• Reason (rational thinking)
• Experience (of Christians, personally and communally).

Creation and revelation

There are two foundational beliefs that shape a Christian worldview. Holding them together helps Christians understand what is the right way to live. But on occasions when one seems more significant than the other, moral choices are more difficult.

The first belief depends on acknowledging that God is the Creator. This is God's world, and it was made for our good. If this is true, then there is a natural order that God has enshrined in the way the world operates, and rational thinking can interpret it. A good life is one that is lived in step with the orderly pattern that God has ordained for all humanity.

The second belief is that God has continually revealed his will to the world throughout history, and most importantly in the person of Jesus. Jesus' teaching about the Kingdom of God (a development of the laws of the Jewish people and amplified by the New Testament letters) establishes a moral foundation.

An example that shows the two beliefs in concord is the Christian conviction that one day in every seven should be a day of rest. This is in sympathy with the natural order of God's creation, in which there is a recognizable rhythm of seasons, fruitful and fallow, in pace with which humans need to work and relax. But it also reflects a command whose origin is revealed in the first pages of Scripture, reinforced by Jesus who affirmed it as God's plan for the good of humans and fulfilled by the selection of Sunday as the day for worship by the first Christians.

An example that shows the two beliefs at variance is the use of condoms in family planning. Roman Catholic theology forbids this, arguing that contraception is contrary to the natural principle that procreation is the conclusion of sexual intercourse. Protestant thought has stressed the revealed intention of God that children should be born into a setting in which they can best receive love, education and material care, suggesting that parents should be actively involved in decisions about the timing of childbirth. The discovery that condoms provide protection against HIV has put this moral dilemma into even sharper focus.

Christians seeking to discern what it means to live a godly life in each succeeding generation hold those two beliefs together with two other criteria – the Christian tradition that has unfolded through the centuries and the experience of believers, personally and communally, of God in action in their world. Those four sources brought together can shape a Christian worldview.

must know

In this century, those who look to the pattern of the created order to seek God's will point out that there is a causal link between the recklessness with which humans waste energy and the increase in flooding that brings acute distress to many of the world's countries. This is a sign, they argue, that the human contribution to global warming is a sin which defies God's intentions for a responsible use of the planet's resources.

Conversely, young people who seek the revealed will of God to shape their worldview might be recognized because of the popularity of wearing wristbands that bear the letters WWJD, standing for 'What would Jesus do?'

Distinctive Christian attitudes

When reason, Scripture, Christian tradition and experience of life are brought together, they provide a lens through which features of the world in which we live can be examined. They help Christians conceive of a world in which men and women are glad to be alive, give and receive love and die feeling that their life has been worthwhile.

must know

Psalm 24 begins:
• The earth is the Lord's, and everything in it, the world, and all who live in it;
for he founded it upon the seas
and established it upon the waters.

The environment

In the myths that begin the Bible, God creates the world from nothing and devolves the care of it to the first humans. Theirs is the responsibility to subdue its wildness and the right to benefit from its fruitfulness. These were duties and privileges that could be used in a stewardly or exploitative way.

Most Christians regard the parlous state of the environment which threatens the future of human life on Earth to be the result of sin, the fracturing of obedient trust between God and humankind referred to as 'the fall'. Ecology reveals a delicate balance of all things animal, vegetable and mineral, which accords with the Bible's vision of *shalom* (a rich Hebrew word that approximately translates as peace) in which God, humankind and nature thrive in harmony. The Bible insists that the world does not belong to men and women; it belongs to God, who will hold humans accountable for the way they have treated it.

It is in that context that Christians have come to regard the wasteful plunder of the planet's resources as the most grave sin of the present age. Addressing the personal sin, there are ambitions (with varying degrees of commitment) to live a simpler lifestyle.

Addressing the institutional sin, there are campaigns to counter the causes of climate change and pollution.

It must be added that many Christians have come late to this cause. There is a belief by some, taking a literal view of parts of the Bible, that the climactic return of Jesus will be followed by the creation of a new heaven and a new earth. It leads to a view that the decline of the planet is of limited importance compared to a divine plan for life throughout eternity (it may even assist God's work by accelerating the new creation). This belief persists in some places. However, Christianity is a religion that has always valued the physical as well as the spiritual. God's command that the inheritance with which he has entrusted each generation should be passed to children and to children's children prevails and compels most Christians into environmental action.

The end of life

A Christian worldview insists that human life is precious, being in the image of God and with capacity for fellowship with him. Everyone has a duty to respect and conserve human life – a responsibility not only to themselves but to their fellow humans.

The Bible is insistent on the utter wrongness of murder, but stresses the inevitability of natural death. So there is no unambiguous implication of a duty to save life at all costs, leading to complex debates about particular circumstances.

Specific protection is demanded for those who, in a godless world, might be considered expendable – the disabled, those too old to look after themselves, and non-combatants innocently caught up in war.

must know

Words from Deuteronomy 8 that hold together human privilege and duty:
• 'God is bringing you into a good land ... a land with wheat and barley, vines and fig trees, pomegranates, olive oil and honey ... you will lack nothing; a land where the rocks are iron and you can dig copper out of the hills. When you have eaten and are satisfied, praise the Lord your God for the good land he has given you. Be careful that you do not forget the Lord your God, failing to observe his commands ... You may say to yourself, "My power and the strength of my hands have produced this wealth for me." But remember the Lord your God, for it is he who gives you the ability to produce wealth.'

However, doctrines have developed in response to tragic cases in which the ending of a life is likely to create the conditions in which others can survive and flourish. Christians do not all agree on the circumstances in which a life lost in the pursuit of a greater good is justified. Two issues that Christians continue to debate are the death penalty and euthanasia.

Capital punishment is present in the Bible, used for exceptional crimes, which convinces some of its necessity. However, the World Council of Churches promotes its abolition, arguing that an irreversible punishment prevents the Christian ends of repentance and reform.

Agonizing experience by some Christians has led them to believe that a person whose continued life will bring them only distress should be allowed to choose the time of its ending through euthanasia. In contrast the hospice movement (pioneered by Christians) draws attention to the pressure on vulnerable people of feeling oneself a burden to family or society. No one who is the object of love, of God or of others, is living a life without value. Mainstream Christian opinion sees these as reasons not to allow intervention in a way that accelerates death, but instead to make the best use of compassion and pain control.

The beginning of life

Belief in the sanctity of human life also generates debate about its beginning, and the point at which the collection of cells from which all life develops begins to be a person. Christian attitudes to issues

---

must know

Psalm 116 speaks of God's care for those coming to the end of their earthly life:
• Precious in the sight of the Lord
is the death of his saints.
O Lord, truly I am your servant;
you have freed me from my chains.

such as abortion and stem-cell research depend on this. The Roman Catholic Church and conservative Christians argue that a human being is brought into existence at conception. This means that an unborn child is one of the vulnerable people whom the Bible singles out specifically for defence in their helplessness. If this is true, then to abort or destroy during a scientific experiment the cells in which there is the potential of life (or even to use contraception to prevent their development) is effectively murder.

A comparatively small group of Christians is more persuaded by the argument that at an early stage a foetus is not viable as a life and is part of a woman's body, the destiny of which she has an absolute right to control.

Most Christians find themselves in the tradition that stretches back to the time of Jesus, which is that children, even unborn, are precious to God and must not be wasted. They press for more stringent abortion laws, especially now that medical advances mean that babies born increasingly early in a pregnancy survive. However, they make exceptions because they understand that the mother herself may be the one who is vulnerable and in need of protection, perhaps because she has been raped or her survival is endangered. They may also find themselves persuaded that medical research using human embryos (by-products of infertility treatment that would otherwise be destroyed, and too young to be recognized as viable lives) is permissible because of its potential to bring an end to chronic diseases that as yet have no cure.

must know

Psalm 8 is typical of the regard in which human life is held in the Bible:
• O Lord, our Lord, how majestic is your name in all the earth! ...
When I consider your heavens, the work of your fingers,
the moon and the stars, which you have set in place,
what are mere mortals that you are mindful of them,
human beings that you care for them?
Yet you made them a little lower than the heavenly beings
and crowned them with glory and honour.

Family

Jesus was brought up in a home that modelled the parent–child relationship regarded in Jewish families as the best setting in which to survive a tough life. His ancestors had lived in tribes of intergenerational support. He himself remained single. His followers around the world 2000 years later live in such varied circumstances that a definition of family is barely possible – nuclear, single-parent and extended families. A Christian worldview seeks to honour all these circumstances as settings in which love can thrive, economic security can be achieved and faith can be nurtured. Family challenges selfishness, provides continuity in times of change, and challenges the view that work is life's only priority.

However, there is realism in a Christian worldview, and a recognition that much damage is done within families (it is actually hard to find a happy family in the Bible). There is division among Christians over whether arrangements that have not historically formed part of the Christian tradition are an acceptable continuation of the ever-widening boundaries that define family, such as polygamous families (a pressing issue in some African churches) or homosexual couples (a pressing issue in some Western churches). However, there is near-universal agreement that those who begin to explore faith while in a family relationship that is not recognized as ideal in the Christian tradition (for instance, a cohabiting couple) should experience welcome in a church, not criticism.

At the heart of a Christian view of family is marriage. In marriage a man and woman leave their families and join together to make a new family, creating a partnership of love, the exclusiveness of which is deepened by sex. It is a covenant forged through promises made before God and witnessed by the community, and is regarded as the best context for nurturing children.

At their wedding a couple make vows that endure until one of them dies. Some Christians believe that this means that marriage is indissoluble, and that even in cases where the couple separates painfully, they are still married from God's point of view. Roman Catholic theology upholds this 'sacramental' view, although occasionally allows a marriage to be declared null (meaning that it never really was a marriage). Protestant and Orthodox churches, attempting to be true to a biblical position that is not precise, have accepted divorce and remarriage in some circumstances – for example, to relieve one partner of intolerable hardship, unfaithfulness or desertion. Christian leaders are called on to show pastoral wisdom in upholding the seriousness of wedding vows while at the same time responding with compassion to deep hurts.

In Christian tradition marriage is also seen as the best (many would say the only) setting for sex. This view struggles to retain credibility in the twenty-first century, ignored by young people outside the Christian community and a formidable challenge for young people inside it. In this context, the positive way in which the Bible describes sex as a generous delight and an expression of commitment has been overshadowed by the impression that it is something with which Christians are not at ease. The nature of sex, with its giving and receiving, its healing and enriching, can be debased by self-gratifying paedophilia or adultery, and the repulsion that is shared inside and outside churches would have a greater impact were it not for some highly publicized instances in which Christians in positions of authority have offended.

Equality

God has conferred immense dignity on the human frame by choosing to walk the earth as a person. Every human is precious to God in identical measure. This is true regardless of gender, age, race, religion, disability, status or sexuality.

The Bible speaks of men and women, members of one human race, both bearing in every way the image of God. It speaks of Abraham, ancestor of the Jews, being the means through which every other people group throughout time should receive God's blessing. It speaks of people who are unable to contribute to the economic prosperity of the community (children, the elderly, the disabled, refugees) being afforded special care.

Historically this has led to Christians worldwide being in the forefront of progress toward the emancipation of women, the abolition of slavery, the end of apartheid, opposition to the stigma attached to leprosy, prison reform and human rights.

Some would point out that the record is patchy. In many denominations principled theological analysis maintains the conclusion that ordination to the priesthood is available only to men. HIV, regardless of how it was contracted, still attracts stigma and judgment in the churches of some countries. In many places there has been little

must know

Galatians 3 insists on the equality of all humans because, in Jesus, God has dignified the human frame:

• 'You are all children of God through faith in Christ Jesus ... There is neither Jew nor Greek, slave nor free, male nor female, for you are all one in Christ Jesus.'

attempt to understand Islam, still less to approach
Muslims as men and women equal in God's sight.
And the ease with which homosexual people have
received acceptance is notably greater in secular
circles than in churches.

Nevertheless, in locations where a church is the
only place that an asylum seeker senses friendship,
or where a prisoner's only visitor is a Christian, belief
in the equality of all humans before God genuinely
inspires action.

Food and drink

There are no laws relating to food and drink to which
Christians are expected to adhere, part of the
freedom that is seen by the New Testament as the
natural consequence of the salvation Jesus has
brought. Specifically this has released Christians
from the restrictions on acceptable foods that
featured in Jewish law and practice. The enduring
principle relating to food and drink is that one
should consider the impact of consuming it on
others. The first such issue dividing Christians was
that butchers placed meat in front of idols before
selling it to the public. Logic dictated that this was a
meaningless act since the gods represented were
non-existent, but it nevertheless offended purists.
Paul was adamant about the freedom of Christians
to eat without constraints, but insisted that it was
appropriate to refrain when in the company of those
for whom it would cause distress.

This leads some Christians, even entire
denominations, to forego meat or alcohol, but in a
context that tolerates the point of view of those who
do not share those convictions. The social and

spiritual significance of food and drink as a God-ordained provision is high in Christian practice. The New Testament encourages both hospitality and fasting, observing that Jesus knew the time for each. However, it rebukes gluttony and drunkenness (taken by most Christians to preclude other drugs), encourages exercise, and insists on the welfare of land and livestock. Maintaining Jewish tradition, Christians usually pray before eating as a thankful acknowledgment of their dependence on God the sustainer.

Poverty

By teaching, 'Blessed are you who are poor, for yours is the kingdom of God; blessed are you who hunger now, for you will be satisfied,' Jesus put the suffering of the poor at the heart of his message. Throughout most of the centuries since Jesus, Christians addressed poverty through personal charity, self-help policies and the organization of local communities in order to respond to their needs. However the twentieth century revealed the scale of the injustices in the world to be vast beyond previous imagining and those traditional responses, although not without meaning, have become hopelessly inadequate. Global forces, steeped in injustice, determine the destiny of the world's poorest people.

Christian people in the developed world now recognize that poverty calls them to move beyond their own resources and to partner with others in order to work for change. It is justice, not charity, that most Christians now seek, understanding that to be fundamental to God's Kingdom. Out of this conviction have grown the campaigning organizations which facilitate action, giving and prayer – equally prominent in the churches' response. Thus Christians have been the mainstay of international campaigns for reform of the rules that have tilted the benefits of world trade toward wealthy nations and cancellation of unpayable debts owed by the world's poorest nations.

Poverty is not evil (there is, after all, a tradition of Christians choosing poverty as part of modelling their lives on Jesus). The evil is the grinding injustice that requires infants in the developing world to die of easily curable diseases in order for a small part of the world to live in comfort. With wealth comes responsibility. Partnership between Christians in the prosperous parts of the world and development organizations in the poorest areas is usually seen as the approach that has most integrity.

Poor Christians often have a profound sense of living the earthly part of their life in the context of eternity, and trust in Heaven as a place of compensation for their suffering. In some poor communities, however, a literal reading of some Bible passages has led Christians to believe that material wealth is the sign of God's blessing. Teaching that unquestioning faith (usually demonstrated by donating money to the church) unlocks generous gifts from God features in some congregations, but is condemned by most as exploitative.

must know

Jesus clearly took inspiration for ministry among the poor from the Old Testament prophets, such as Amos 5:
• 'I know how many are your offences and how great your sins.
You oppress the righteous and take bribes and you deprive the poor of justice in the courts ...
I hate, I despise your religious feasts; I cannot stand your assemblies ...
Away with the noise of your songs! I will not listen to the music of your harps.
But let justice roll on like a river, righteousness like a never-failing stream!'

Violence and peacemaking

Christians follow a leader who declined the opportunity to lead an armed uprising, instead choosing to submit to brutality without resisting – a path that led to the salvation of humankind. The Christian worldview is absolutely set against violence. However, there are considerable difficulties for the Christian in upholding this. In the first place, the Bible (particularly the Old Testament) portrays a God who encourages violence in order to establish the Jews in a secure homeland. And Christians also have to face up to their own history, for their predecessors waged war in the name of Jesus in a way which is usually recalled with shame. In our own age, Christian commitment to non-violence as an ideal is challenged by the existence of evils so intractable that only military force seems to hold out hope of bringing them to an end. Terrorism and nuclear weaponry have only served to intensify the debate.

A 'just war' theory was propounded by the North African bishop Augustine in the fourth century and has guided Christians subsequently. It lays down five conditions under which the usual rule of non-violence might have to be set aside:

• The decision must be made by the highest possible governmental body (in recent decades most Christian countries have looked to the United Nations for moral authority).

• There must be just cause. It is forbidden to go to war to expand territory, gain mineral resources or dominate others. Just causes are defensive ones, responding to tyranny.

- Every conceivable method to resolve the crisis by peaceful means must have been exhausted.
- A judgment must be made that the war will not unleash more evils than are already being endured.
- And there is a group of conditions about how the war is fought: there must be a reasonable chance of success, it must stop when justice has been restored, the means by which it is waged must match the severity of the injustice and civilians must be protected from direct attack.

A dynamic tradition of Christian pacifism still offers an alternative viewpoint (notably led by Quakers). Advocates of these principles point out that all Christians were pacifists for the religion's first four centuries, and that Jesus propounded not submissiveness, but a kind of militant non-violence which is active, defiant and costly.

want to know more?
- *New Dictionary of Christian Ethics and Pastoral Theology*, David Atkinson and David Field, Inter-Varsity Press, 1995

9 Issues that preoccupy Christians today

Throughout the world the number of Christians is growing at a phenomenal rate. However, the growth is not evenly spread through the world, and in places where Christianity has historically been a strong presence numbers of active worshippers are declining. The centre of gravity of the Christian world has moved from Europe to the developing world. With this change has come a new set of issues that Christians must face, and there is not always agreement about what churches should do to respond to them in a godly way. This chapter examines the concerns that preoccupy believers worldwide as they seek to follow Jesus faithfully in the twenty-first century.

Issues looking inward

The rise of extremism and the distraction of materialism have diminished the ability of Christianity to enrich people's lives. However, issues relating to sexuality have emerged as the churches' most acute dilemma.

Diminishing congregations in European churches

At the turn of the century, the number of Christians in the world was rising at a rate of some 68,000 each day. However, it is in the developing world that the majority of this growth has come. The pattern in European churches is one of diminishing attendance, with 4–8 per cent of the population worshipping weekly. In the USA, 20 per cent of the population go to church on a Sunday.

Ironies are apparent in the UK, where over two thirds of the population identify themselves as Christian, but only a fraction of these have a meaningful engagement with a church. The emerging pattern is of a smaller number of churches with large, lively congregations drawn from all ages, while the majority sustain declining congregations of people in the second half of their lives. Churches are thriving where there has been an impact from immigration (particularly of Pentecostal and Roman Catholic Christians), evangelistic activity (especially initiatives that have the cultural relevance of their activity at the heart of their concern to serve their neighbourhoods) and engaging provision for children and young people.

must know

Worldwide, 130,000 new members swell Christianity every day, one fifth by conversion and four fifths through being born into the faith. At the same time 62,000 leave the Christian faith, approximately one sixth because they convert to another religion or lose their faith altogether, the rest through death. (Statistics from Christian Research)

The rise of fundamentalism

Fundamentalism is a rising tide in all religions. In Christianity it expresses itself in a desire to adhere to the teachings of the Bible in a manner as close as possible to the circumstances of the very first Christians.

This has an impact on fundamentalists' understanding of how the world began: rejecting recent scientific explanations about the evolution of human life, they argue that the world was created relatively recently, and literally in the manner described in the Bible's opening chapters. It also impacts on how they believe the world will end (for which they offer a clear sequence of calamitous events, from which true Christians will be spared by transfer to Heaven, culminating in the majestic return of Jesus). It arms them with uncompromising views of sexual and medical morality, expressing itself in extreme cases in violence against doctors who practise abortion.

Fundamentalist Christianity also has a very negative view of the worth and culture of other religions. Because there has been a similar rise in fundamentalism in other faiths, tensions run high in places where adherents of different religions live in proximity. Only a small percentage of Protestant churches are fundamentalist, but they have an influence that exceeds their numbers. Loyal to their high-profile leaders, they have espoused a political agenda. In the USA, this has allowed them to become influential, shaping education and foreign policy. Some see this as a major challenge to international stability and peace.

must know

Fundamentalists are not the same as evangelicals. This common confusion grieves evangelicals who, although they share a passion for the Bible, insist that it is opened up to critical thinking in the light of scientific, archaeological and literary research. Evangelicals, particularly in the UK, have a positive view of contemporary culture (which they have significantly shaped over recent centuries); they do not consider it to be in the grip of evil, but as something to engage with and influence with Jesus' values.

Homosexuality

Increased understanding of the scientific and social roots of homosexual orientation reveal it to be given by nature and, according to some Christians, therefore given by God. Believers who prioritize the natural order of God's creation in shaping their moral framework have come to the conclusion that faithful, loving gay relationships are blessed by God. However, this opinion has to be defended against the fact that it overturns an almost unbroken history of opposition to homosexuality in the Bible and Christian tradition. Those with a liberal theology (led by some Christians in the UK and the USA) urge recognition of the propriety of homosexual partnerships through services that bless vows of commitment and the acceptance of gay clergy. Those with a conservative theology (led by some African Christians and Orthodox and Catholic leaders) maintain that all sexual activity outside the context of heterosexual marriage is sinful. So entrenched have opinions become that this issue threatens the unity of Christians more bitterly than any theological disagreement of recent centuries.

Polygamy

In Africa, men and women are coming to a Christian faith in large numbers. Some of them come from traditions in which the need for survival has made polygamy a normal part of the culture. When missionaries first brought Christianity to Africa there was an attempt to move abruptly from polygamy to the monogamy on which the New Testament insists. The damage caused by obligatory divorces was considerable and a more pastorally constructive approach is now sought. There is agreement that church leaders should model and teach monogamy as an ideal. But African churches are divided between those who seek to accommodate polygamous practices (using Old Testament examples as part of their argument) and those who resist such moves. The HIV pandemic, which is particularly acute in sub-Saharan Africa, has refocused attention on this issue.

Changing leadership roles of women

The apostles were all male, but women figured in Jesus' ministry in a way that was untypical of cultural conventions. In the churches described in the New Testament there were women in significant positions of leadership, but for the majority of Christian history men have dominated leadership of churches. This partly reflects the fact that most other powerful institutions also favoured male leaders, and partly rises from a strand in New Testament teaching that compares a man to a head and a woman to a body (a metaphor also used to describe the relationship of Jesus and the church).

Changing perceptions of the place of women in society during the twentieth century have caused churches to question whether their practice reflects the intention of God for all time, or has been inhibited by the cultural circumstances of the first century. Ordination remains open only to men in Orthodox and Roman Catholic churches (which go further by insisting that clergy should be single and therefore celibate). Denominations that read the Bible with a very conservative perspective, such as Brethren and some Pentecostal denominations, also insist that the teaching which gives direction to their congregations should come only from men.

In contrast, the Salvation Army has encouraged female preachers from its earliest days, and during the twentieth century a gradual process that led to the full ordination of women took place in the Church of Scotland, the Methodist Church and many other Protestant denominations. Change was slower in the Anglican churches. Florence Li Tim-Oi was ordained by the bishop of Hong Kong in 1944, but it was a further 50 years before there were female priests in the Church of England, and it is still not permissible in certain provinces. Some Church of England Christians are unable to accept the legitimacy of women priests, and a compromise has allowed them to remain in the Anglican Church under the oversight of bishops who share their convictions. Now a pressing and divisive issue within Anglicanism (as well as other denominations) is whether women should become bishops.

Issues looking outward

The relationship that Christians have with those who do not share their faith has become a growing concern as distant parts of the world become less remote. But the biggest health issue faced by the world's population does not discriminate between religious beliefs, and its impact on churches has been formidable.

Interfaith initiatives

Just as once the pagan religions that predominated in the UK had to decide how best to accommodate Christianity arriving among them, so now Christians are aware that followers of other faiths (perhaps 6 per cent of the population) are their immediate neighbours. In other countries the proportions are more equal and the question of how the religions relate is even more pressing. Travel, migration and television have swept away the ignorant assumptions of centuries past that adherents of non-Christian faiths were benighted or wicked. People of goodwill in different religions have been able to work together effectively to reach a common mind on issues such as racism and poverty. They can also agree to urge moderation – not fundamentalism – in their desire for peace.

However, at some point in their desire to relate, members of different faith groups have to tackle questions of truth, even though that is not easy. It is understanding and not agreement that is usually the objective of interfaith dialogue. It is imperative that the various faiths are true to themselves, rather than downgrading the importance of central tenets of their belief.

The need for peace in the lands of Jesus' birth

Violence, oppression and fear have figured repeatedly in the story of the lands in which Jesus lived – before him, after him and particularly in the present day. Christians respond fervently to the Bible's plea to 'pray for the peace of Jerusalem', but there is disagreement about the most appropriate way to see justice done for all its inhabitants.

Fundamentalist Christians read the Old Testament's insistence that the land east of the Mediterranean is the Jews' Promised Land as an indication that the present secular state of Israel has God's authority to control the area. In its extreme form, this view is compounded by the belief that Jewish occupation of the land – even if it means the expulsion of Palestinians – will trigger the longed-for return of Jesus. This view has impacted on political decisions since the Holocaust, but has damaged the aspirations of Palestinians to rise from poverty and determine their own future.

Other Christians interpret the Bible in different ways, either seeing the Christian church as the new embodiment of the privileges and responsibilities once held by God's chosen people, or using a theology of liberation to argue for freedom from oppression for all whose land is occupied, including those living in the Palestinian territories. For people with these views, the violence that has grown out of the inability of Arabs and Jews, Palestinians and Israelis, to live as neighbours is profoundly dismaying. Revered as 'the Holy Land' by Christians around the world, it remains a place of pilgrimage, but Palestinian Christians have felt forced to leave in large numbers in recent years.

must know

From Isaiah 2:
• 'Come, let us go up to the mountain of the Lord ...
He will judge between the nations
and will settle disputes for many peoples.
They will beat their swords into ploughshares
and their spears into pruning hooks.
Nation will not take up sword against nation,
nor will they train for war anymore.
Come ... let us walk in the light of the Lord.'

Personal faith is
something that cannot be
forced, taught or
inherited; it can only be
experienced. What you
need to know about
Christianity can only truly
be discovered by opening
yourself to the possibility
that an encounter with
Jesus Christ might be
transforming. A hymn
written about 150 years
ago still offers words of
hope and devotion that
are a fine way to attempt
to begin a journey of faith:

'O Jesus, I have promised
to serve you to the end;
Now be forever near me,
my master and my friend;
I shall not fear the battle if
you are by my side,
Nor wander from the
pathway if you will be my
guide.

So let me see your
footprints, and in them
plant my own;
My hope to follow duly is
in your strength alone.
O guide me, call me, draw
me, uphold me to the end;
And then in Heaven
receive me, my Saviour
and my friend.'

HIV

The rapid rise of HIV and the vast number of deaths
associated with AIDS have presented the church
with extensive moral and pastoral challenges.
Suggestions in the early years of the virus that those
who contracted it were suffering the consequences
of immoral behaviour have been superseded as the
scale of infection passing from mother to baby or
husband to wife has been realized. The virus is on
the increase in Europe and in some African
countries a quarter of the population is HIV-positive.

The churches' customary teaching about
sexually transmitted diseases (faithfulness inside
and abstinence outside marriage) has not had any
impact on rates of transmission. Some have
responded by advocating the use of condoms (even
distributing them) on the grounds that Jesus taught
that preventing death is a higher priority than
unyielding insistence on obedience to religious laws.
Others (significantly including Roman Catholic
churches) have redoubled their opposition to
condoms and their promotion of celibacy.

Notably in Asia and Africa, churches
overwhelmed by the scale of the epidemic have led
education, opposition to stigmatization and care for
those who are gravely ill. But the virus has robbed
them of the generation that worked hardest and
raised children, so the circumstances in which they
seek to hold out a gospel of hope are severe.

The rise of aggressive atheism

A recent phenomenon of the cultural life of the UK
has been a rise in militant atheism. Arguing either
from a scientific or a sociological perspective,

commentators attacking religious belief as if it were not just meaningless, but poisonous, have become familiar through books and newspapers. Opposition to the influence that Christians have in public life is sometimes expressed through campaigns to remove the Christian foundation from schools, or to end the presence of senior bishops in Parliament. Because it is couched in language that is sometimes ferocious, it does not distinguish between religious extremism and the temperate influence of Christian faith in the everyday working of society.

Christians in the UK now have a context of hostility in which to make their case for allowing the love of God, displayed in Jesus, to shape the world. But after decades in which the message has been launched on to a sea of indifference, there is much evidence of the churches being galvanized by the challenge of bearing witness to Jesus in the provocative new circumstances.

want to know more?
● *Issues Facing Christians Today*, John Stott, Zondervan, 2006

Further reading

Bibles:
New International Version, Hodder and
Stoughton, 1973
New Revised Standard Version, HarperCollins,
1989

General:
David Atkinson and David Field, *New Dictionary
of Christian Ethics and Pastoral Theology*,
Inter-Varsity Press, 1995
David Barrett (ed.), *World Christian
Encyclopaedia*, Oxford University Press, 2007
Mary Batchelor, *The Lion Book of Christian Poetry*,
Lion Hudson, 2005
Pope Benedict XVI, *Jesus of Nazareth*,
Bloomsbury, 2007
Paul Cavill and Heather Ward, *The Christian
Tradition in English Literature*, Zondervan,
2007
John Drane, *Introducing the New Testament*,
Lion Hudson, 1999
–*Introducing the Old Testament*,
Lion Hudson, 2000
Gordon Fee and Douglas Stuart,*How to Read the
Bible for All It's Worth*, Scripture Union, 1994
Peter Graystone, *Detox Your Spiritual Life*,
Canterbury Press, 2004
Jonathan Hill, *The History of Christianity*, Lion
Handbooks, 2007
CS Lewis, *Mere Christianity*, HarperCollins, 2001
Neil MacGregor and Erika Langmuir, *Seeing
Salvation*, BBC Books, 2000
Timothy Radcliffe,*What is the Point of Being a
Christian?*, Continuum, 2005
The SPCK Book of Christian Prayer, SPCK, 1995
John Stott, *Issues Facing Christians Today*,
Zondervan, 2006
Richard Taylor, *How to Read a Church*, Rider,
2003
Tom Wright, *Simply Christian*, SPCK, 2006
Phillip Yancey, *The Jesus I Never Knew*,
Zondervan, 2002

Useful websites:
www.biblegateway.com
www.christianity. org.uk
www.findachurch. co.uk
www.life4seekers. co.uk
www.rejesus.co.uk
www.religionfacts.com

Glossary

Agnostic Someone who concludes that it is not possible to know whether or not there is a God.

Amen A word meaning 'Let it be so,' commonly used at the end of a prayer.

Anglican communion A worldwide fellowship of churches in a close relationship with the Church of England.

Anglo-Catholic A tradition within Anglicanism that has practices similar to Roman Catholicism.

Apocrypha Books associated with the Bible, recognised as part of Scripture by some, but not others.

Apostle One of the twelve originally chosen by Jesus, and their successors who were sent to spread his message.

Atheist Someone who firmly concludes that there is no God.

Atonement The action that brings people into a life-giving relationship with God.

Baptism An action that recognizes new membership of the church through sprinkling with or immersion in water.

Born again One way of describing the Holy Spirit's action when a person comes to faith in Jesus.

Byzantine Churches east of the Mediterranean centred on Constantinople (Byzantium) which are in the Orthodox tradition.

Canon The list of books that was recognized in the fourth century as being part of the Bible.

Catholic Meaning 'universal' when it describes the whole church, it is sometimes used to shorten Roman Catholic or Anglo-Catholic.

Charismatic Someone who emphasizes the importance of the Holy Spirit in Christian life and worship.

Christ Meaning 'anointed one' in Greek, this was the leader who was expected to lead the Jews to freedom.

Christening The giving of a name when a child is baptized as an infant.

Communion Or 'holy communion' - a service at which bread and wine is consumed in remembrance of Jesus.

Confirmation A service at which those who were baptised as children affirm as adults their intention to follow Jesus, at which they symbolically receive the Holy Spirit.

Covenant Meaning 'agreement' or 'deal', this is the pledge of God to a special relationship with his people.

Creed A formal statement of belief.

Denomination An organized grouping of congregations which have similar beliefs and structures.

Ecclesiastical Relating to the church.

Ecumenical Working for the unity of all Christians, particularly bringing denominations together.

Epistle A letter in the New Testament.

Eucharist Meaning 'thanksgiving', another word for communion.

Evangelical A tradition of belief that values the Bible very highly and stresses the importance of a personal relationship with Jesus.

Evangelism Spreading the good news of God's love revealed in Jesus. (Roman Catholics sometimes substitute the word 'evangelization'.)

Exegesis Studying the meaning of the Bible to its original hearers.

Gentile Someone who is not Jewish.

Gifts of the Spirit Abilities given by the Holy Spirit to Christians to allow them to serve each other and the world.

Gnostic Someone having the belief that salvation can be attained through secret knowledge.

Gospel The good news of what God has done through Jesus.

Grace The superabundant love of God, given without cost, conditions or favour.

Heresy A teaching that subverts mainstream Christian belief.

Hermeneutics Interpretation of the Bible to make clear its relevance to the present day.

Holiness A quality describing God, revealing him to be completely set apart from anything impure. Objects associated with God are also described as holy, and Christians are called to be so.

Holy Spirit The personal presence of God at work in the world.

Icon An image of Jesus or a saint revered in Orthodox worship.

Image of God The humane and creative part of a person that shows the characteristics of God.

Incarnation The action of God in inhabiting human flesh in the person of Jesus.

Glossary

Intercession A prayer for a particular person or event.

Judgment The moment at which all humans are called to account for their deeds, faced by Christians with confidence because of Jesus' actions on their behalf.

Justification Acquittal from anything that would prevent a person being united with God.

Kingdom of God The place where God's rule is made perfect, revealed now because of Jesus, but destined to be established immoveably in the future. Also known as the Kingdom of Heaven.

Liberal theology A stream of theology that questions the Christian tradition and insists that a changing culture must be met by a changing faith.

Liberation theology A stream of theology that sees the good news through the eyes of poor and oppressed communities, especially in Latin America.

Liturgy A set order of worship.

Mass Meaning 'sent out', the word Roman Catholics use for communion.

Messiah Meaning 'anointed one' in Hebrew, this was the leader who was expected to lead the Jews to freedom.

Ministry Service of any kind done in the name of God to benefit the church or society.

Missionary Anyone who works to fulfil God's plan for the world, but particularly used of those who explain what God has done through Jesus in contexts where that is unknown.

Monotheism The belief that there is one God – central to Islam and Judaism as well as Christianity.

Myth A timeless story which may or may not be factually true, but which reveals powerful spiritual truths.

Original sin A worldwide climate of wrongdoing that is the context in which Christians make their moral choices.

Orthodox churches Churches belonging to the oldest tradition of Christian practice.

Passion The suffering and death of Jesus.

Pentecostal churches Churches belonging to the tradition that emphasizes experience of the Holy Spirit.

Pharisee A sect of Judaism at the time of Jesus that adhered strictly to religious laws.

Proselytize Encourage someone to convert to Christianity from another religion or from no active faith.

Protestant churches Churches that belong to the tradition founded at the time of the Reformation, stressing the Bible's authority.

Redemption A metaphor taken from slavery that speaks of the freedom that Jesus has won through his death and resurrection.

Reformation The sixteenth-century movement that culminated in reform and division in the worldwide church.

Repentance Literally, 'a change of direction' in order to follow Jesus.

Roman Catholic churches Churches that belong to the largest denomination, looking to the pope as their leader.

Sabbath A day to rest from work and reflect on God, usually marked by Christians on a Sunday.

Sacrament A sign that represents an action of God too powerful for words. Baptism and communion are widely recognized by Christians, and Roman Catholics have five others.

Saint Taken to mean a person of exceptional holiness whose prayers reinforce those of Christians. In the New Testament, all Christian people are called saints.

Salvation The rescue of a person from sin, death and meaninglessness.

Schism A separation between two groups of Christians on a matter of principle.

Second coming The belief that Jesus will return to earth as its Lord, ending the present age and ushering in a perfect eternity.

Speaking in tongues Using languages unknown to the speaker in praise of God, or as a message from God.

Synoptic Gospels The Gospels of Matthew, Mark and Luke, which have striking similarities.

Testament Literally meaning 'covenant', the Old and New Testaments form the Bible.

Theology The study of God, academic or informal.

Tradition The aspects of Christian faith that are passed on from generation to generation.

Trinity One God, Father, Son and Spirit, faith in whom is Christianity's distinctive belief.

Virgin birth Belief that the conception of Jesus took place through the intervention of the Holy Spirit while Mary was a virgin.

Yahweh The holiest name of God, used frequently in the Old Testament.

Index

Index

Index